FRUIT AND VEGETABLE GARDENING FOR BEGINNERS

2 BOOKS IN 1:

THE BEST TECHNIQUES AND SECRETS TO GROWING YOUR OWN FRUITS, VEGETABLES, AND HERBS IN THE HOME GARDEN

Bradley Gray

2

including any legal fees potentially resulting from the application of any of the information provided by this book. This disclaimer applies to any loss, damages or injury caused by the use and application, whether directly or indirectly, of any advice or information presented, whether for breach of contract, tort, negligence, personal injury, criminal intent, or under any other cause of action.

You agree to accept all risks of using the information presented inside this book.

You agree that by continuing to read this book, where appropriate and/or necessary, you shall consult a professional (including but not limited to your doctor, attorney, or financial advisor or such other advisor as needed) before using any of the suggested remedies, techniques, or information in this book.

Table of Contents: Fruit Gardening for Beginners

Table of Contents: Vegetable Gardening for Beginners

FRUIT GARDENING FOR BEGINNERS

THE BEST TECHNIQUES AND SECRETS TO GROWING YOUR OWN FRUITS IN THE HOME GARDEN

Bradley Gray

Introduction

Gardening can be rewarding in many ways. There are a lot of different approaches that result in different achievements. Before deciding how you would like to garden, you should understand what limitations you have and what you hope to get out of your gardening experience.

There are so many incentives for gardening. It might be for wholesome, fresh produce; for some peace of mind or stress release, or just because it is something your family has always done. If your doctor advised you to take up something that will keep you active and you're not into sports, take up gardening. You will never regret your decision.

There is never a wrong reason to garden. It is a hobby that gives back to everyone involved, including the environment.

Gardening can add to the beauty of your land. It can give your home that curb appeal you have always wanted. Adding color to a bland patch of grass can help to warm things to a new level.

It is highly beneficial to start gardening to lessen your grocery bill. A garden can give you fresh fruits, vegetables, and herbs for free. You will have a small amount of start-up money and some labor. You will also have fewer trips to the grocery store if you get a good crop growing.

Gardening can be very therapeutic for some people. The routine of doing the work can make them feel more energetic and disconnected from all the things that cause stress in our lives. There is also a gratifying feeling at seeing your results. Regardless of what those results are, you will be a success because you will have learned a lot from your experience. Things you will want to repeat and things you will not want to repeat. All are valuable lessons.

People have different intentions for gardening. They are often limited by their living arrangements. When you are ready to decide the style of gardening you are going to use, it is important to consider whether you want to arrange your garden indoors or outdoors. Outdoor locations might be limited due to sunshine exposure and drainage. The amount of space you must work with might help to decide your technique. The area you live in will help you to think about what you must work with. Your weather might cause problems or limit you to certain timing. It will also be helpful to recognize what you are trying to gain with gardening. You could just want an escape. It's possible you just want fresh produce. What a great reason!

All Methods of Gardening Share These Same Benefits

Two often unanticipated benefits of gardening are its delightful connection to nature and its remarkable stress-relief side effect.

Connection to Nature

Gardening is taking your place in nature. You are working with natural elements to bring forth delicious and nutritious produce to be eaten by your household. After you start gardening, you will feel more in touch with life outside your home. The insects, breeze, rain, and all other elements of Mother Nature will start to become more noticeable to you. You might be out at a friend's house and hear the thunder. Normally, you might think nothing of it. Since you have been gardening, you might think, "I hope my tomatoes can make it through a storm." Gardening will also allow you to escape the technology of the world. It allows you to stop and smell the roses. You can leave that cell phone in the house and take a short, electronic vacation. If you take the time and dedication, you can enjoy the smells, sounds, and colors of your garden. It generates a reason for you to get off the couch and go outside.

Stress Relief

People often garden for stress relief. It can be very therapeutic. The act of doing the responsibilities gardening requires can relax the mind. It is easy to get outside and enjoy the fresh air. The change in pace can allow your mind to clear and relieve you from the everyday issues we get stuck thinking about.

The pride in the success of a garden can make the work less of a chore and more enjoyable. The physical activity required releases endorphins, which in turn release a lot of tension built up from our everyday lives. You can be getting a large amount of exercise without even realizing it. You will also be getting sunlight, i.e., vitamin D, which is great for your health. It's a free vitamin D day when you garden. Soak up the sunshine and enjoy your new-found passion.

Chapter 1: Where to Start?

Start small. It's good to get excited and think about how you may develop many distinct sorts of products, however, you'll get overwhelmed if you tackle an excessive amount. In your first year, start small to enjoy and research what works for you, after which you may extend in the years to come. This is likewise a less high-priced manner to get started.

Plan What to Develop

When making plans for what to develop, it's crucial to pick out meals that your circle of relatives will eat as well as clean plants that don't require a lot of unique care. You'll additionally want to keep in mind your neighborhood conditions, consisting of the season, usual weather, and solar exposure. You can discover more about your neighborhood developing sector and usual first and closing frost dates by doing internet research of your region.

Figure Out the Nice Site

Pick a nice site on your lawn, whether it's a few bins, a raised mattress, a sunny region interior close to a window, or an area to position a vertical lawn. Be positive and keep in mind how much sunlight the site receives based on what you intend to develop. Additionally, you need your lawn to be positioned near a water source, your gardening tools, and your kitchen. To put together the site, you could take away grass, smooth up or flow vintage flowers, or tidy up your patio, deck, or a sunny spot interior to make room.

Decide on What You'll Develop In

In element 2, you'll discover ways to construct a few clean raised beds or planters. But in case you don't have the time or ability to do this, you could purchase a raised mattress package and, whether you're developing interior or outdoors, use character bins and planters. Even better, you could develop your flowers in recycled family bins in case you are in a decent price range or need to be more sustainable.

Build High-Satisfactory Soil

The high-satisfactory and fitness of the soil you are working on immediately influences how properly your flowers will do. When you're beginning out, it's crucial to shop for the proper soil and upload natural amendments to it over time. This is the premise for what we call "constructing your soil." Avoid the usage of lawn soil for bins; it does now no longer drain properly and is regularly too heavy for bins consisting of placing baskets. Instead, use potting soil, that's lighter. If you choose to go with hydroponic, you won't even want soil! How a lot less complicated can you get?

Plant Seedlings or Begin Seeds

For a beginner, shopping for seedlings at a nursery or lawn middle is the perfect manner to get started. However, in case you need to develop a specific type of veggie that your lawn keep doesn't have, you could additionally begin your flowers with the aid of using seeds. When the seedlings get large enough, you'll transplant them into your raised mattress or bins so that they can develop large and strong.

Establish A Weekly Gardening Schedule

To gain achievements with your city lawn, you'll want to know when you'll have time to work on it. This doesn't take all weekend. All you want are a couple of minutes right here and there all through the week to maintain matters, after which an hour or so at the weekend will help you do several longer tasks. Even when you have a hectic lifestyle, fundamentals consisting of watering, fertilizing, weeding, controlling pests, and pruning won't take up an excessive amount of your time. Gardening enables you and your circle of relatives to loosen up and gradually relax after a hectic day or week.

Deal with Troubles

You must address troubles on your lawn, and you also want the proper mindset to address them and discover solutions. This is the primary reason why a few novices quit. Plants may get sick, be broken due to neighborhood wildlife, war in the soil or conditions, or appeal to pests. The crucial issue isn't always to get discouraged. Even the maximum pro gardeners run into trouble. They have simply found out how to address them.

Harvest!

This is the praise for all your difficult work. The first time you choose that sparkling tomato or harvest a few lettuce leaves for a sandwich is awesome. You do want to test your veggies as they develop so that you don't end up with zucchini the size of a baseball bat! And when you have kids, that is the precise assignment to delegate to them—if you could maintain them from ingesting the entirety at the spot.

Understand Your Local Regulations

You might assume that developing meals at home is something that nobody has issues with. After all, you're doing an awesome thing, right?

Unfortunately, it's now no longer continually so clean. There are policies and rules you want to observe; otherwise, you chance dropping your lawn or being fined.

Every town or municipality has positive bylaws that manipulate what you're allowed to do for your property. These cowl fence height, accent buildings, smells and noises, and ugly premises. Before you begin your city lawn, make sure to study through the files that apply to you.

If you stay in a network with a homeowner's association (HOA), keep in mind that a few don't permit any meal gardens, even in the backyard. Check the policies and rules carefully. If your HOA does permit meal gardens, they'll be particular about the kinds of beds and bins you're allowed to apply, so your lawn doesn't detract from your neighbors' amusement or the aesthetics of the entire neighborhood.

If you rent, test together along with your landlord before you dig up the entire backyard! You can be constrained to the usage of a balcony, a deck, a patio, or an indoor area. If you do get a few areas in the backyard, keep in mind that someday you could want to transport and will lose your flowers.

Even if you observe all legal guidelines and rules, from time to time, the best thing to do is talk to your neighbors. Let them understand some of your plans for developing meals and cope with any of their questions and issues before you get started. Maybe they'll get the meal-developing bug, too!

Essential Tools for A Fruit Garden

Many of the things that you want are probably already around your home – especially if you're working on different outdoor jobs.

Here's a brief listing of a few helpful gardening equipment:

- Gloves can help you avoid hand blisters. Cotton gloves will be the most affordable, however, more luxurious gloves manufactured from sheep and goats last longer.

- A great straw hat with a wide brim can keep the sunshine off your face while letting in air to help keep you cool.

- A pocketknife or set of pruning shears is great for slicing side strings and blossoms.

- Sturdy rubber boots, lawn clogs, or boots repel water and deliver resources for digging.

- Bug repellent and sunscreen to keep you comfy and steady while working on the lawn.

<u>Watering Hoses and Cans</u>

Plants require water to grow, and when Mother Nature isn't cooperating, you may need to water frequently. For a large lawn, you would require fancy soaker hoses, sprinklers, and drip irrigation pipes. However, for plenty of small residence gardeners, a simple hose and watering can can work wonders.

Rubber hoses kink less compared to nylon or plastic pads; however, they may be a lot heavier to move around. Whatever fabric you choose, make sure to procure a hose that is long enough to reach flowers in each region of your lawn while not having to take water containers to reach more remote flowers. Decide on a hose that incorporates brass fittings and a washing machine included in the hose; some additions make the hose less probable to fail after extended usage.

Watering cans may be crafted from easy, cheap, brightly colored plastic or fancy metal. Vinyl is lighter; however, galvanized metal is rustproof and more appealing. Watering cans are available in many sizes, so it is best to know which size you need before purchasing. Ensure it is easy to cast off the sprinkler head for cleanup.

Hand Cultivators

A 3-pronged hand cultivator is a beneficial device to cut up clods of soil, straightforward seedbeds, and function in granular fertilizer. Additionally, after you plant your little box or extended mattress, a cultivator is a first-rate device to remove younger weeds as they germinate. When you're digging a planting hole, then a hand cultivator divides the floor easily in comparison to a hand trowel. Much like a hand trowel, make sure you choose a hand cultivator that feels cushy for your fingers as it incorporates a grip firmly fixed to the blade. The metal-bladed sort may last longer.

Spades and Shovels

Spades and shovels are simply part of the most-used gardening gears. A spade can be used for grinding as well as scooping and projecting. Shovels historically have curved and pointed blades, while spades have flat, right, almost rotating blades. A first-rate spade is crucial in any lawn for dispensing dust, manure, or compost. A spade is essential for trimming or breaking a sparkling floor. Many gardeners use spades for anything from slicing dust bags to hammering in bets. Very proper spades are rocky. Spades and shovels can either be long or short. A longer handle offers you greater leverage while digging holes, so keep this in mind in case you are shopping for a brand-new spade.

Garden Forks

Since a spade is for turning new lawn dust, I discovered that an iron fork is a much better device for turning beds that had previously been worked on. The fork sinks into the ground in as deep as 12 inches, it divides clods, and it loosens and aerates the soil more than a shovel. Iron forks look like short-handled spades aside from the 3 to 4 iron tines on their heads. The best ones may be those with 1 piece of metal with timber grips firmly connected. They are not only used for turning dust, but also for turning compost piles and root crops, like carrots and potatoes.

Garden Rakes

When you dig soil, you need to stage it, split clods of soil, and smooth the seedbeds (especially if you're creating raised beds). An iron rake is the best device for the process, though you can only use it in some instances. A 14-inch-diameter iron-toothed rake should have a lengthy, wooden cope that is securely connected to a metalhead. You might also additionally flip the metal head to ease a seedbed stage. Look for an aluminum rake to get a lightweight though a less-lasting model of an iron rake.

Buckets, Wagons, and (Additionally) Baskets

Though you don't own a 1,000-rectangular-foot lawn, you still need to move around seeds, fertilizer, gear, crates, and more. Listed under are three essential packing containers:

- **Buckets**: For potting soil, fertilizers, and hand gear, a 5-gallon plastic bucket is a first-rate box. You may obtain one from a construction site, so make sure you wash it out nicely. To get a greater, long-lasting albeit smaller bucket, then buy one constructed from galvanized metal.

- **Wagons**: For lighter items, like packets of seedlings, you can use something like a kid's old purple wagon. Wagons are first-rate for moving flowers and small bags of compost for your lawn. The wagon bed also allows you to preserve this stuff in the area – this is better than leaving it on the bumpy floor. If you're thinking about a wagon to move yourself (instead of gear) across the lawn, a brand-new innovation is using a chair as a saddle. This type of wagon usually has a swiveling chair and can be perched on four analog wheels, letting you take a seat down and push yourself which lets you move at some point on the lawn. Its storage area is beneath the chair.

- **Baskets**: To acquire the best thing that will help you expand your harvest, invest in a cable or wicker basket. Wire baskets are less complicated to use as it is feasible to scrub the product whilst it's nevertheless from the basket. Wicker and wood baskets are great as they are aesthetically appealing and last even longer than those made of metal. Using a basket to pile in all your harvest is a lot better than trying to carry all the zucchini you have on your hands; it will also be easier for you to move them from your garden to your kitchen.

Wheelbarrows and Garden Carts

There will come a time where you need to move heavy things such as soil and fertilizer from one area to another for your garden or lawn. The best thing for moving stuff that is "bigger than a breadbox" are wheelbarrows and garden carts. The easiest way to distinguish the two cars is by using their wheels. Wheelbarrows have a single wheel together with an oval, alloy tray; garden carts have four wheels and a square wooden tray. Wheelbarrows are maneuverable in tight areas, can turn on a dime, and can dump things easily. A contractor-kind wheelbarrow has a deeper tray – this is worth the extra funding because of its first-rate quality. To get a light-weight wheelbarrow, look for one with a tray crafted from plastic. Garden carts are a lot higher, can move around larger things, and are less complicated to push than wheelbarrows. A large-sized garden cart can move around hundreds of soil, gravel, stone, and bales of hay without a problem. Some lawn carts have removable rear panels which make dumping less difficult.

Power Tillers

The traditional back- or front-tined energy tiller evolved to large-scale anglers which are now used by gardeners to turn their gardens during autumn and spring. The large power tillers (more than a 5-horsepower motor) are best when you have 1,000 rectangular feet or longer to till. Additionally, they may be essential for forming raised beds and dividing sod.

Chapter 2: What Is the Best Soil?

Add three parts of compost and one part of manure on any soil you have at your disposal. After that, rake the soil, break all the clumps, and ensure the surface is level.

Soil, sun, and water are the most important elements of gardening. Poor-quality soil can affect all the efforts you poured into your garden. Choosing first-rate soil is extremely important. What makes up a high-quality soil ideal for gardening?

Premium soil is well-aerated soil. This means that air has appropriately circulated through the soil giving it a healthy and bouncy feel. Soil that is too thick will not give the roots a proper chance to grow. Dense soils, like clay, will not make room for adequate water drainage as well.

Healthy soil should be free of other materials, like stones, that tend to obstruct growth. Sandy soil is a poor choice for a hearty garden. First-rate soil must be rich in organic matter, like ripened manure or compost.

You can make your compost by collecting peelings, pruning wastes, fallen flower heads, and even old tea bags and newspapers. These can all be turned into compost that's rich in nutrients. Just fill your compost bin with a mixture of brown and green materials and deposit it into your garden. Permacultures of worms and bacteria will grow into the bin. Mix the compost into your garden soil and the soil will nourish your plants.

There is also a different way of improving your soil through compost. Just deposit barks and leaf molds into the soil where worms and the weather can work their way in. Compost is the answer to soils that couldn't hold moisture well or to soils that are too thick. Fertilizers will, eventually, be unnecessary.

The ideal season to prepare your bed soil is in autumn. Prepare your plot by digging not more than 8 inches into the ground. Begin by loosening the soil. Remove all destructive materials like rocks and large woods. Start incorporating your organic compost into the soil.

Now all you have to do is wait for the next spring when planting starts.

The Best Potting Soil

If you're considering planting flowers for your lawn or developing your garden for flowers, you need to recognize which soil is exceptional for plant boom. The sort of soil you have on your lawn depends on where you're living, and it should simply be different from your neighbor's. This is because you should have exceptional soil to grow flowers. Additionally, you can know how great a certain type of soil is depending on the number of flowers growing on it.

Let's talk about outdoor and indoor soils so you can see the difference between them, and you can determine for yourself the exceptional ground for the boom of flowers.

Outdoor Soils

Outdoor soils are usually of 3 distinct types:

- Sand

- Clay

- Sand or silt

The best soil for flowers is one that is wealthy in vitamins, and this is sandy soil. However, don't feel bad if you think your soil does not meet the suitable situations; you could constantly alter its characteristics and turn it into top-quality soil with a touch of fertilizer.

Indoor Soil

If you've got flowers that are growing indoors, you may think that it will be a great idea to move the soil out onto your lawn and have your flowers grow there. However, that is a mistake and is additionally a horrific thought.

Garden soil incorporates microorganisms that could kill your houseplants. There are other alternatives in case you don't want to use the potting soil being sold in stores; you can sterilize the ground outdoors.

Sterilize the Outdoor Soil

If you choose to move your indoor flowers outside, you should first sterilize the soil to get rid of illnesses and remove bugs and weeds. After purifying the ground, you should alter the soil with peat and sand, so your flowers can have good drainage and the proper air so that there is ideal humidity.

You also can pick to shop for potting soil as they're very comparable and extra snug for your flowers. These soils encompass peat moss and vermiculite, which is a gradual launch of fertilizers appropriate for the boom of your flowers.

Both components will assist your flowers in developing robust roots due to the fact they'll be capable of reaping vitamins, humidity, and ventilation.

Know the Types of Soil for Your Garden

To acquire a dream lawn or have a well-stored nook of lush flowers, it's critical that you recognize the sorts of soil, their traits, and are aware of which one you want for every plant. The characteristics of the land are crucial!

Choosing the proper substrate is likewise critical for your plants to grow correctly. Each sort of soil has its specific bodily and chemical traits, and in the market, you could get numerous types depending on the specific needs of your plant.

A substrate could make your flowers more resilient against pests and different factors that could preclude their growth, besides defending them from parasitic illnesses.

Would you want to analyze what kind of land you've got for cultivation and which of them are more suitable for your plant type? Everything you're analyzing will be very beneficial.

- **Prepared Land**

It is the perfect substrate for pots because they have correct water drainage. In general, prepared soil is the only one used for the exceptional boom of decorative flowers in pots, planters, flower beds, and gardens.

Prepared land is most known for instantly growing a brand-new plant in a pot; this way, you could expect its top-quality from the beginning.

This sort of land contains additives, with the well-known ones being washed water, compost, moss, and rice husk.

- **Professional Land**

This sort of soil improves moisture retention and turns on herbal plant safety systems. It is a substrate that incorporates good-sized possibilities of nitrogen, an excellent detail for developing flowers. It additionally has an aggregate of black peat, peat moss, granules, and perlite. When is it beneficial? Professional substrates may be utilized in any crop, both indoors and outdoors.

Among the benefits of the use of this substrate is the plant could be healthier and more resistant to illnesses. Another benefit is that it is suitable for the basic improvement of flowers as the stems could grow to be more robust.

In summary, when you purchase professional land, your flowers can expect a higher metabolism and a low occurrence of illnesses. This fact will imply larger, stronger, and leafier plants.

- **Black Earth**

Black soil tends to be very uniform and is suggested for grasses and pots. Black earth is prominent precisely through its color (darkish black) and its origin (it becomes shaped after the decomposition of natural matter). Black soil is usually made from remnants of dry leaves, or the natural waste of animals that are absorbed as vitamins through the soil.

This sort of soil may be very beneficial while creating a crop or planting flowers. It is extensively used for the sowing of decorative flowers or additionally for the cultivation of food plants. Black earth performs an essential position as it incorporates vital vitamins in vegetables or fruits.

There are many benefits of black earth; however, we will point out its herbal potential to hold sufficient water for the improvement of the plant. Also, its additives are best for the circulation of the roots; in this way, the plant's growth is top-quality and wholesome.

- **Potting Soil Substrate**

It is good for foliage, vegetation, and veggies as it incorporates an excessive range of vitamins. The substrate is one of the primary sources for flowers as it provides fertility to the soil and vitamins to the plant. Thanks to the substrate, various issues regarding the growth of flowers may be avoided.

Among the sorts of substrates, we will especially highlight natural substrates and inert substrates. Among the natural substrates, one of the best is earthworm humus, a sort of substrate that gives more fertility to the soil due to its specific composition: nitrogen, phosphorus, potassium, calcium, magnesium, iron, and sodium, amongst different factors.

Furthermore, this substrate can inhibit the improvement of fungi and microorganisms that could affect flowers. Another of the exceptional recognized natural substrates is mulch, a sort of substrate this is liable for stopping early erosion, and still gives natural substances to the earth that help it battle against excessive or low temperatures.

Coconut fiber, perlite, gravel, and sand are in the category of inert substrates. This set of substrates has the perfect additives to nourish flowers. It also allows for the correct drainage of the soil and preserves the proper humidity for the flowers' improvement.

- **Leafy Ground**

Leafy soil improves soil texture and lets in a higher quantity of air. This type is taken into consideration as the "black gold" of flowers as it can offer a huge variety of vitamins (micronutrients and macronutrients).

Using it will result in your flowers being capable of germinating higher, their boom being a lot faster, and they will look stronger. By the time you decide to feature leaf soil for your vegetation, you may be routinely enhancing the composition of the ground, in addition to enriching it with several vitamins.

- **Organic Land**

Organic soil improves moisture retention and offers more resistance to the plant. A fantastic gain is that it can be used on all sorts of flowers. Organic soil is a part of the fertilizer that flowers must receive if you want to make their boom healthier.

Some professional gardeners use it as a lawn filler since this sort of soil can enhance the variety of vitamins in the land.

- **Special Lands**

Some special lands, because of their composition, are best in certain sorts of vegetation. This includes orchids. These soils can offer the vitamins that flowers need to appear beautiful, with green leaves and brightly colored plants.

Do you understand what sort of land to pick? Beautifying a lawn is more than directly planting a few flowers and watering them from time to time. If you need wholesome and robust decorative flowers, the soil is critical to acquiring that goal. The diet of a plant and the absorption of vitamins will depend on the quality of the soil you've purchased, so you'll want to shop for the proper substrate.

Having a lawn, land, flowers, and vegetation in first-rate situations isn't impossible; it starts through selecting the proper soil and with the appropriate composition. It gets a whole lot easier as you watch your little plant develop and grow stronger day by day.

Chapter 3: The "Lasagna" Method

The Dig Less Gardening, better known as DLG, isn't about getting rich off "Texas tea" from the ground. DLG is about becoming wealthy by learning about and then harnessing some of the true richness of the soil. DLG is all about becoming prosperous while working with nature rather than against it.

I've profited from the skills I've acquired over the past many years as a gardener. The food I've eaten, the nutrition, and the exercise are connected deeper with the root of this world, the true wealth of the living soil. Hopefully, this little DLG guide will provide others with some keys to unlocking and harnessing the power that exists in a healthy living earth.

DLG is a no-till or zero tillage operation over the life of a garden. DLG is about disturbing the soil as little as possible once the DLG is built. The goal is to do as little interference with the inhabitants of the soil by mimicking mature. In return, the rewards reaped include getting healthy plants for a healthier MBS and the health of the whole Earth.

Some people will ask "what's the point of Dig Less Gardening?" Hopefully, this book will help answer some of the many questions that can be raised by people that aren't familiar with a DLG approach to gardening. I think some of the answers to the question happen to be the many positive aspects when it comes to DLG, a form of no-dig or no-till sheet mulching style of gardening. One of the goals is about not disturbing the soil in the growing beds as little as possible so the life in the soil can do what it is meant to do.

People will often say they don't have a green thumb when it comes to gardening. Instead, they say they have a brown thumb. In the Dig Less Approach, a brown thumb is what is needed. This gardening technique is a twofold approach. First, there is the how-to construction part of a DLG garden. Secondly, and most importantly, is the brown thumb side working with the soil. If a gardener plays their cards right, the world that lives in the soil beneath us will do much - if not most - of the work for us. Once the DLG microbe palace is constructed, the microbe angels and saints of the underworld will work their magic.

DLG uses a simple technique that some might call lasagna or sheet mulching style vegetable gardening. That's where layers of organic materials are placed on a kill-mulch ground cover and then planted in. The ground cover used in DLG is cardboard.

Instead of digging up or tilling a lawn or other patch of Earth with vegetation like an established vegetable garden or some sort of patch of weeds, DLG might meet your needs. Often, using what is called a no-dig or no-till approach can be an awesome way to start a garden or move from a conventional dig and till gardening. In this Dig Less Gardening approach, gardeners can learn and then lean into this technique and turn away from digging and tilling the soil. Starting small and getting comfortable with the DLG approach is a good idea. Then with more familiarity, the use of DLG could be possibly expanded as the need arises.

Dig Less Gardening is intended as an introduction for the potential gardener that would like to learn how to grow vegetables without tilling or digging the soil. The techniques covered here are simple enough steps and inexpensive, but each step does take some time and energy as it includes gathering and installing the materials. Once the appropriate items, like cardboard, organic materials, compost, etc., are collected, the project can move forward rather rapidly. A DLG could be considered as a landscape installation project. That's because DLG is about building something lasting that can be productive year after year if attention is paid, to some basic construction and later maintenance practices after building the DLG.

A DLG is a sort of a permaculture-type garden arrangement. In other words, all the work that you put into the construction of the DLG pays off big time because you won't need to do as much in the future after the construction phase is completed. Once the DLG is put together and is up and running it's more like a perpetual growing machine. With some care, a DLG will provide healthy fruits and vegetables not only for many years but also contribute in a positive healthy fashion to larger issues the Earth faces like carbon sequestration.

After the DLG is put together and growing great food from the healthy creation, you'll hopefully find there is often less maintenance with things like weeding. That can be a winner for people that don't enjoy weeding.

Season one with a DLG is about construction, planting, and growing, and allowing the new garden to settle in with the Earth it rests on. Like a wine that can improve with age, a DLG should also slowly but surely develop and increase its health and wealth. In short, once the microbe temple is built, offerings are made at the altar in the form of carbon, the food of the microbe gods. Happy healthy Soil critters can equal happy healthy plants, healthy people, and a healthy Earth. Can I type that line too much? I think not!

This guide isn't just for novice gardeners. DLG offers a great deal to more advanced seasoned growers. DLG is a how-to lean into kicking the destructive conventional techniques and practices of scorched Earth gardening of tilling, digging, and nuking the Soil life. Hopefully, prospective readers will be comfortable and learn enough to try some of the Dig Less Gardening approaches.

Most of us only know about digging, turning, tilling the soil, and then planting. This Dig Less Gardening how-to guide is here to help introduce novices and others to the concept that tilling is not necessary, plus some of the multitude of benefits to the soil, plants, nutrition, and climate change. In many situations digging into the soil is no longer required to grow a vegetable garden. In some cases, people that own a rototiller will find they can eventually sell this dinosaur. After learning about and then reaping the rewards after trying out the Dig Less Gardening approach, the soil can change, the plants can change, we can change, and the Earth can be changed for the better simply by raising healthy vibrant soil and tasty awesome food.

Most people think they need to race off to a store of some sort and haul a bunch of fertilizer home to feed the plants they grow in their garden. That might be the case in traditional scorched Earth gardening but not so in DLG. With a little knowledge and a well-put-together DLG, feeding the garden carbon in the form of mulch and or compost should keep the microbes whistling while they work in the smorgasbord of carbon you provide and they get to chow down on. In a nutshell, the life in the soil eats the vitals that you provide as well as minerals in the soil, and they feed the plants and the plants feed the life soil all over again. They work together, bartering in a give and take sort of way. If we choose to work together with the soil-plant combo, we are all winners. The soil-plants, MBS, and Earth all gain in positive ways.

There is discussion today that many human illnesses, modern-day plagues, can be attributed to human's disconnection from the healthy microbes of the Earth. If this is turning out to be the case, and I believe it is, DLG provides an unparalleled health spa. Not only can a DLG provide nutritious food but also when we garden in healthy living Soil our body and microbes that make us what we are all happier campers. Happier campers can help create and maintain a happier world.

To wrap it up: Dig Less Gardening is a win-win gardening approach for novice and most other gardeners that would like to learn how to do sheet mulching, lasagna style, no-dig, no-till, fewer weeds gardening. Learn to create a traditional row layout garden where a lawn or other vegetation is or has been growing. Learn how to convert a lawn or other ground like a tilled garden into a Dig Less Gardening for fruits and vegetables. Plus, the big winner is of course health and wealth for the trilogy of the soil-plant, MBS, and Earth.

This K.I.S.S. (Keep It Simple Stupid) approach isn't limited to the creation of a square or rectangular vegetable row and mound garden. With some creative thinking and work, Dig Less Gardening can be adopted by gardeners to be a variety of shapes and for many different types of planting and garden styles and layouts.

This guide covers some things like, what is Dig Less Gardening, why Dig Less, benefits, equipment needed, how-to steps, tips and resources, and more.

Chapter 4: The Display of Your Garden

Deciding on which plant to grow will depend on your taste and suitability to the environment. Study the plants first so you won't regret what you planted. Stronger plants have greater immunity to pests and diseases. However, are they apt for your soil and location? As much as possible, always choose the varieties that are disease resistant and have strong soil compatibility.

Maybe you can plant something exotic that's not available in your farmer's market. Plant the vegetables and fruits that you find pricey or have poor quality in your local grocery store. Organic produce is especially expensive in the market. Grow them in your backyard and expect some major savings. Don't forget the freshness and tastiness that's always available in your kitchen.

You can start with packets of seeds or with seedlings that started in the greenhouse's nursery. Seedlings are more costly than seeds but it's a great choice for beginners. Seedlings will save you time. If you are choosing seeds, be sure to read the labels and instructions about watering and spacing. Labels will also tell you if you can directly sow the seeds into the soil or if it needs to start indoors. You can grow ample seedlings indoors while waiting to plant outdoors. Choose plants that appeal to your diet and be sure that they are suitable for your garden's size.

Types of Garden

Deciding where to grow your garden is an important task. This is where your plants will live and where you'll watch them thrive. The first consideration is always the sun. Where does the sunlight hit the most? That is where your garden will be. There are three types of garden you can choose from. Decide on one that will support your needs and lifestyle.

A traditional garden is a kind that will give you tons of options on plants that you can grow. The natural soil beds will help you utilize and maximize the nutrients found in the ecosystem. Though some insects and bacteria can help the growth of your plants, some bacteria varieties may be the deterrent factors. If pests and microbes develop into a problem, control them naturally. There are safe and biological controls available like microscopic worms which are effective in killing vine weevil grubs.

If you are an apartment dweller in the city, a traditional in-ground garden may be impossible. It's best to choose container gardening as an alternative. Several container types that vary in size, shape, and material are available in the market. There is no limit on the type of container you can use. The conventional clay pots and terra cotta are the most popular ones, but you can also employ recycled materials such as wooden barrels, old bottles, plastic containers, or galvanized metal buckets. Since space is the foreboding factor, you can try planter boxes on your windowsills or even hanging planters. Wall planting has become a revolutionary and ingenious technique in urban gardening.

When considering the container types, bear in mind their differences. Some can retain heat while some may lose moisture rapidly. Poke a few holes if you're aiming for DIY planters to ensure adequate drainage. Choose a container deep enough for the roots. If you are using organic potting soil from the store, container gardening is the best choice. Store-bought soil is already rich in nutrients, weed-free, and has aerated. Choose plants that are suitable for such a limited space and place them right where the sunlight is. Plants that are ideal for container gardening are spinach, lettuce, garlic, onions, green beans, carrots, and herbs. Tomatoes and peppers are also suitable, but they require staking for they will outgrow the container.

If you're looking for something that's between traditional gardening and container gardening, raised beds are your options. Raised-bed gardens let you control weed growth. It's also the perfect solution for gardeners who want to limit their physical movements and for those who are suffering from back problems.

Bricks, cinder blocks, rocks, and untreated wood are used to raise the garden beds. The height of the raised beds can range from 6 inches off the ground to two or three feet. Depth should be at least 16 inches. The width shouldn't be more than four feet to make sure that you can still reach the center. Raised-bed gardens are as good as traditional gardens. You can grow any plant using high-quality soil. Even deep-rooted vegetables like cabbages do well in raised beds.

Since the early days of man, plants have always been a natural part of our life. For many reasons, humans have always taken gardening as a choice activity, both for sustenance and for recreation. The beauty that comes with the natural gifts of having healthy greenery in our environment is another factor that endears man to gardening. Every time space permits, people are quick to start a garden in their backyards, the yard, or a field. From the strength that comes with the natural build of a fruit tree to the shade it provides, to the yearly expression of beautiful colors and the tranquility of a garden, all these factors contribute to creating a strong bond between man and his garden, not forgetting the savory taste of garden products.

The close links that man has managed to create with nature naturally are also a very important part of yards and gardens. Not only do we take our time to tend to our gardens, but we also pay keen attention to them to make sure they are healthy and well sanitized. With the right amount of space, you can convert your lawn to a pleasant haven of healthy vegetables, fruits, and herbs for either commercial use or domestic consumption. You may also incorporate a range of shrub plantings in your outdoor garden.

You may also have an outdoor garden in a limited space. Hanging baskets, container gardens, raised beds, etc., are ways of incorporating healthy plants into your garden to create a beautiful ambiance that gives life to the outer space of your home.

If you wish to venture into outdoor gardening, you must bear in mind that there are a lot of conditions and activities that come with this venture. You will need to deal with pests, weeds, and diseases. First, you need to get valuable knowledge on the best outdoor gardening practices. Get the most suitable crops for your location and opt for the healthiest varieties of plants. You also need to find the best outdoor vegetables, fruits, and herbs that will best contribute to helping you choose the best outdoor garden designs, or layouts but note that you are going to combine all these factors with dealing with the perks of outdoor gardening.

Outdoor Gardening

Physical and Mental Well-Being: Outdoor gardening is a very beneficial venture for one's overall health and maintains a healthy mind and body. Because of the activities or exercises that come with maintaining an outdoor garden, many people, especially seniors, turn to it as a recreational activity to cleanse the mind and keep the body fit. Outdoor Gardening involves a lot of physical activities. As you plant, pull out weeds, and dig, you get the chance to burn up to 400 calories every hour. This will not only help you to stay fit; your brain and mind will also stay sharp.

It has also been proven to be a great stress reliever, reduce blood pressure and cholesterol, as well as ease depression. According to studies, just looking at plants can result in changes in the heart, blood pressure, muscle tension, and electrical activities in the brain. When they play with colors and textures, gardeners can imbibe emotions of peace, tranquility, and joy. It is safe to say that gardening goes beyond mere recreation, as it also serves therapeutic purposes for the soul and body.

Environmental Benefits: These days, we tend to hear more about the effects of the activities of man on the environment, but little is often said about the great benefits of the green impacts of gardens to the earth. Just as it is with indoor gardens, the plants in outdoor gardens also serve as air purifiers as they take in carbon dioxide and other air pollutants and produce oxygen. Plants also produce fragrance. Other benefits of outdoor gardening to the environment come from such factors as plant covers like mulch, which keeps the soil firm. As a result, soil erosion is reduced, keeping sediment away from streams, drains, and roads.

When you plant new outdoor gardens like rain gardens, you will be making use of the run-offs from rainwater, such that harmful pollutants never make it to streams and other water bodies. Not only are traditional outdoor gardens like rain gardens good for the environment, but they also need less maintenance, and as such, they cost little funds. Let's not forget that these gardens are also very beautiful and pleasing to the eyes.

Beyond the benefits that outdoor gardens have for the environment, there are benefits of outdoor gardens that are important to man's well-being. It has been discovered that when you have a proper environmental landscape design, it will keep your home cool during summer and warm it up during winter. There are also energy-friendly landscapes which, according to the Plants for Clean Air Council, can help reduce energy costs up to 20%.

Increase the Value of Properties: You also get the chance to invest in the future by maintaining a beautiful outdoor garden landscape design. When your garden is designed beautifully, it makes your entire house more beautiful and appealing. This will also boost the whole value of your house. The monetary value that the garden can add to your house to help you sell your house faster than it would have been the case with a house without a garden.

Growing Green: Not to be cliché, but we always hear the phrase, "seeing is believing." If you are growing for commercial purposes, it will be easier for your potential customers to see what you are selling to them; the plants' freshness, and the quality of what they get from you. Rather than using artificial nutrients and light, as is the case with indoor garden practices, you can guarantee organic farming in your outdoor garden as the plants readily have everything they need available to them from nature. In this case, you are sure of what your herbs, fruits, and vegetables have touched, what they consume, and how they grow.

Self-Satisfaction: Outdoor gardening has gone beyond a mere activity for survival to become an art. Just as the diverse landscape styles that come with outdoor gardening can add beauty to your home, it is also a great satisfaction source. The land and space you use for your outdoor garden also afford you the chance to explore and try out a lot of new plants and styles. As you continue to practice, you will keep getting better at what you do, such that you begin to see new opportunities and exploit them as they come.

Types of Outdoor Gardens

When one speaks of an outdoor garden, the general notion may be the image of plants scattered across the place. The truth is that there's more to outdoor gardening than just putting seeds into the soil. Outdoor gardens come in many shapes and sizes, and they can comfortably accommodate different types of plants at the same time. Don't make the mistake of thinking of the outdoor garden as just flower or vegetable gardens. There is more to the outdoor garden. As you already know, plants are very good ways of added beauty and color to your home, both inside and outside the house. This is probably why more and more people continue to embrace gardening every passing year. It is important to correct the misconception that gardening is only about typical residential or commercial landscapes because, in truth, various types of gardening have to do with different styles, methods, locations, and plant varieties.

Outdoor gardens are generally divided into two broad types, namely, the ornamental and food gardens. The ornamental gardens are of different types according to the variety of plants grown in them and the methods used in arranging those plants. The most popular types of ornamental gardens are container gardens, rock gardens, wildflower gardens, formal flower gardens, informal flower gardens, and water gardens. A few of the things you will typically see in these gardens are shrubs, grasses, and trees.

Ornamental Gardens

Ornamental gardening is planting that involves growing different plants in one place for aesthetics. This system of gardening is designed to form a beautiful pattern for viewing pleasure. The first aim of this gardening is for aesthetics. The area where ornamental gardens are planted are designed to add beauty to the environment; hence gardeners that are into this system are not very concerned about crop production. In creating landscaping plans, ornamental plants are often incorporated into the designs, and as such, many states create ornamental gardens to attract tourists and for the viewing pleasure of those who live in such cities.

While this ancient practice is mostly used for flower gardens, the modern practice has found ways of incorporating food crops into this system, so ornamental gardens may also include vegetables, herbs, and fruits. It is natural for humans to want to create beautiful pieces for pleasure and relaxation, but it is also important to eat healthy foods. This is why gardeners have now found a way of planting food crops without leaving aesthetics behind. This system of gardening is simply the proverbial way of using a stone to kill two birds.

Gardeners now use food crops to form ornamental gardens around their homes, in public places like churches, galleries, or any other place dedicated to meditation. Imagine a beautiful garden where you can find orange fruits and savor the fresh scent of herbs. It is important to note that some religions have spiritual activities that are meant to take place in gardens, while other gardens of this type are meant to serve recreational purposes.

It is important to note that there's no standard layout for ornamental gardens. They may differ according to the types of plants grown and the environmental factors that surround the garden's location. While a few of these gardens may be highly majestic with an intricate arrangement of beds and lanes that are more appealing when sighted from afar, others like those meant to beautify small cottages are done in a very casual style.

The extent of ornamental gardens' beauty cannot be overemphasized, but beyond its beauty, one cannot neglect how useful these gardens can be. For ornamental gardens with fruits, herbs, and vegetables, one cannot ignore the fact that the products are very healthy, while typical ornamental gardens can serve as recreational spaces for sports, lounging, strolling, theater, or live musical performances. One may use such gardens for events like birthday parties, weddings, etc. as the garden's surroundings go a long way to add to the beautiful ambiance of the events.

Ornamental Fruits, Herbs, and Vegetables

When you opt for an ornamental vegetable, herb, and/or fruit garden, you get a brilliant burst of colors in your garden and your foods as well. One of the best reasons why ornamental edibles are becoming a favorite is that children can also get involved in the gardening process. They can join in the harvesting process, and they also get to eat healthy vegetables without resistance thanks to their vibrant colors. Studies have also shown that the colorful pigmentation that produces the colors has antioxidants that help guard humans against diseases.

Although the idea of maintaining edible ornamental gardens is not entirely new, it has continued to become more popular. In the past, we've had gardeners incorporate herbs into different parts of their outdoor flower beds. The truth remains that edible plants, regardless of where and how you choose to grow them, are never chosen as ornamentals before they are chosen as food. The first aim of growing herbs, vegetables, or fruits is to consume them as food. When they are used in ornamental gardens, they serve both purposes, and in that case, nothing is lost as many of the typical ornamental vegetables also act as decorative edibles. You may push to achieve both aesthetic pleasure and feeding pleasure with your garden without losing out in any aspect. All you need to do is to get proper knowledge of how this is done and invest quality time to get it done as well,

You will not be surprised if you find a gardener mixing both vegetables and herbs in the same container or garden bed. In an ornamental garden, this is often done by combining vegetable and herb plants with similar colors and textures to complement the rest of the garden's color scheme. To give a better boost to the beauty of your edible ornamental garden, you may choose to plant your crops in raised garden beds such that they are easily accessible. This will also give room for a better drainage system. Having a circular garden is another choice.

A wide range of vegetables may be added to the ornamental garden to give it an appealing look. These fruits and vegetables may be planted in containers or garden beds. If you plant appealing leafy fruits and vegetables in your garden, you will have a very interesting garden in terms of looks. The good news is that there are very many varieties of greens in this category to choose from. From the many shades of red hues, greens, purples, and bronzes to the fire red textures or the red sails; think about the loose-leaf lettuce that introduces the red-bronze color into the garden or the Cimarron lettuce, which invites more bronze to the garden. Rather than planting ordinary green romaine, you may opt for freckles as this variety is dotted with burgundy and immune to bolts, just like the darker variant of the burgundy Galactic, which has curled leaf edges. Rainbow chard is another beautiful plant that you may want to add to your ornamental garden as it comes in many colors. There is another form of chard known as the Bright Light. This type of chard comes with colorful stems and leaf veins of purple-red, orange, hot pink, red, and yellow. Thanks to its length, it also serves as a colorful backdrop for other plants.

If you are looking to add more colors to your garden, Carmen sweet peppers are a beautiful addition that could give your garden a burst of colors. This pepper comes in different colors, shapes, and sizes, so pepper lovers have a wide range to choose from. You may go for the greenish, purplish, whitish, reddish, yellowish, etc., variety as they are always readily available within a broad spectrum of colors.

To incorporate fruits into your ornamental garden, you may look towards popular vegetable fruits like eggplant. This plant also comes in many colors from greenish white, to dark purple, to pink or lavender. You may also find a few of these plants with stripped varieties.

One good way of adding vibrant colors to your garden's landscape is to plant tomatoes, with their bright cherry red fruit, which also has many varieties. You may get the purple, black, white, yellow, red, or the stripped variety. Another practical choice is the bean plant, which you may not know also comes in different colors. Try to get the purple or the yellowish-green beans to add more color to your garden. Remember the colorful bean blossom? This should be good for you. The ornamental scarlet runner bean blossom, which comes in a bright pink color, will give life to where it is planted.

The cabbage plant comes in different shapes and colors, just like cauliflower and broccoli. You may find the odd-looking orange cauliflower or the purple broccoli. As odd as they may look, they may be the plants that will invite your non-vegetable-eating family members to dinner. The perennials like the globe artichoke are plants that are likely to add diversity to your garden. With its beautiful leaves and attractive fruits that transform into hallucinogenic, blue-colored fruits that invite bees from a long distance, you definitely will want to stay back and stare at your garden for a long while. Try asparagus as well. With its lengthy, wispy fronds that look like ferns, you will succeed in creating a cool, beautiful edible garden. If you are in this for the long haul, rhubarb comes back to the garden each year by spreading its large leaves over the scarlet stalks that spring from the soil and are a viable choice too.

Another good news is that you can successfully grow plants like lavender as ornamentals and medicine. With its purplish-blue flowers, this plant grows in clusters and can serve many purposes for domestic and commercial use. Consider making essential oils, perfume, and indoor decoration from the product of your beautiful garden.

Food Garden

The food garden is the most common outdoor garden for growing herbs, fruits, and vegetables. Here, farmers use different techniques to grow, hone, and cultivate plants for domestic or commercial purposes. In many cases, fruit trees like apple or pear trees are used to enclose the garden space. In other cases, barbed wires or stakes are installed around the garden to form a fence around it. Many of these gardens are also left without barriers. It all depends on the gardener's choice. Within the barriers (inside the garden) are fruits, herbs, or vegetables planted in different styles on ground-level or raised beds. When planted on raised beds, the soil is given a chance to warm up during the early days of spring. The raised beds are also easier to keep. The crops in food gardens are planted in ways that are easy to maintain, even without synthetic pesticides. All that is required is the availability of organic matter and organic gardening techniques or other beneficial cultural methods like companion planting, crop rotation, or mulching. All these techniques are employed for the healthy growth or cultivation of food crops.

Other Outdoor Garden Types

Rock Garden

You may not have a large expanse of land with fertile soil on a flat plane to plant your crops. This may be a luxury in a few areas. Therefore there are other alternatives, like the rock garden, an option for a sloppy area. This is also a great alternative for locations where the water supply may not always be available. A rock garden is also a practical choice for people who desire to bring the desert's sparser beauty to their homes. Some plants do well when planted on rocks or gravels. Such plants create a unique beauty when planted in such conditions. Plants like the desert. Aloe vera plants do well when they are planted in such environments under warm temperatures. If you are resident in an area where the weather is mostly cold, you may go for plants that require cold temperatures like the ice plants, etc.

Water Garden

This is another outdoor garden that can bring the peace and tranquility associated with nature to one's home. This gardening involves a water body like a pond or a stream within one's location, and many plants grow and thrive by or in water. The peaceful ambiance that the presence of water bodies brings, can be both soothing and refreshing, and this can also endear certain animals to your space. You may then choose to match this serenity up with highly appealing plants by choosing from your variety of fruits, herbs, and vegetables. All you need to do is make sure that your chosen plant will survive in such a condition.

Community Gardens

Community gardens are public spaces given up to individuals to rent a portion of land where they can plant their herbs, fruits, and vegetables for domestic consumption or commercial purposes. These gardens allow people to get fresh farm products, even though they don't have lands of their own where they can grow crops. Ornamental gardens may also be planted in this space to beautify it and bring life to the neighborhood by giving residents a feeling of being connected to their environment. The care of these gardens is done collectively, and everyone who participates in taking care of the garden shares the products.

With such a garden, all individuals involved are given a sense of productivity as they get to share in the chain of food production. It is important to note that these gardens are not merely for growing vegetables, fruits, and herbs, as there is also room for planting native crops and medicinal herbs. There are also butterflies and ornamental gardens of this type. A community ornamental garden is often a public place for the display of the artistic beauty of plants.

Outdoor Gardening Methods/Layouts

Container Gardens

Container gardens open gardeners to an entirely different style of gardening, as opposed to the traditional gardening style. With this gardening style, farmers get the chance to move their plants from one spot to the other to get the desired nutrient. Container gardens are mostly used indoors, but they are also used to plant crops outside. This gardening method takes away the problem of dealing with weeds and other soil-borne plant diseases. Gardeners can also control the moisture level of their plants, and they can decide the level of sunlight and temperature that their plants are exposed to.

There is also the perfect chance to recycle with this method using items that are no longer useful in the home. Industrial materials that may have been abandoned or thrown into a landfill can also be used.

You may decide to use old boots, old buckets, or an old bathtub for this purpose.

Container plants may be placed individually in the outdoor garden or aligned in groups to add a beautiful look to the farm. These containers may be of different sizes, shapes, colors, and textures. The same goes for plants. The aim is to create a beautiful appeal on the farm using these containers.

Raised Bed Gardens

Just as is the case with container gardens, raised bed gardens help gardeners control the type, quantity, and quality of soil used in the garden. Because raised beds are often isolated structures made up of either concrete, wood, or stone, the soil underneath doesn't always affect the garden's outcome. With these structures, gardeners can plant medicinal, edible, and ornamental plants using unusual surfaces like rocks, hard clay, or even concrete surfaces. They give room for proper drainage and maintain the temperature of the soil. One factor that endears this system of gardening to people is the fact that it does not cost so much to maintain, unlike the traditional gardens.

According to the gardener's desires, the planks used in building raised beds are either screwed or nailed in different sizes and shapes. The standard practice is to make to have a relatively wide bed but making sure that the width is not too much. This is to help the gardener to reach the plants in the raised beds comfortably. The heights of the raised bed are typically about three to eight inches high, depending on the nature of plants grown in them. Good, healthy soil is used to fill raised beds. Compost and prepared manure are also mixed with the soil to give it a healthy boost for the plants. Elderly gardeners and the physically challenged use this system of gardening more because they can access it from a vantage point according to the bed's height. They can also sit while tending to their garden, so their joints and spine are not stressed or strained.

Tire Gardening

There is an appeal that comes with using recycled tires in the garden. The use of these tires also adds beauty to the idea of container gardening. To use tires as containers for your garden, simply get an old tire, and remove the outer rim to make it flexible. You may also work the tire's tread by pulling it out from the inside. This will give a visible, sleek look to it. The next step is to stack up treads, one after the other, to put the tires in perfect shape for planting. You may grow potatoes or other root plants in this container as it allows for enough space for the roots to spread. If your plant is the type that requires warm environments to grow, the black surface of the tire gives the best chance for warmth.

If you don't want the natural circular shape of tires, you can alter its shape by tweaking it into your desired shape. All you need to do is to get logs and fix them into the tire to give you the shape you want.

Rows

This is the most popular outdoor garden layout, which has a straight design achieved with long rows that span from the left to the right side of the garden. With the left, the right direction of the rows, the garden is exposed to adequate sunlight and perfect circulation of air. If the rows are directed in an east to west position, it becomes too shaded such that the plants grown in the other rows don't get enough sunlight and air.

When growing crops in rows, it is advised that you grow tall plants like corn or beans on the northern end so that they don't end up forming shade over small plants. On the other hand, taller plants like tomatoes are meant to be grown in the middle of the row, while the short crops like the carrot plants are to be situated in the southern part of the garden.

Square Foot Garden

The square foot garden structure is made up of grids that are 4x4 squares. The grids are characterized by either woods or strings fixed to the frame for dividing the bed into equal-sized sections. Each section houses one kind of vegetable, herb, or plant; the number of plants contained in each section must be calculated. This is done by dividing the least number of spacing inches required by 12. This will typically give you the size of a single plot. For example, if the closest space between your onion plants is usually about three inches, your calculation will automatically become 12 divides by 3. This will give you 4, the exact size of a plot. This means that four rows in a plot will have four plants, such that you have 16 onion plants all together in a plot.

Vertical

Just as it is with the indoor gardens, you can also grow vertical plants in your outdoor garden. This is a good layout for a person that does not have enough lawn space to practice every other layout or method. Instead of using the traditional system of having garden beds, you can use up the vertical space by planting crops along either trellis, by using hanging baskets, or hanging your plants upside down. You may also use stackable containers to help you grow plants in a particular part of your garden by placing pots on one another to create a structure like a tower. These are called planting towers, and they are used as vertical options for planting root crops like potatoes.

Chapter 5: Easier Fruit Plants to Grow

Growing Your Fruit

Growing your food is both satisfying and gratifying, not to mention a cost-effective way of putting healthy, eco-friendly food on your table.

There is a wide variety of plants to choose from. We will look at the selection of potentially viable fruits best suited for raised bed gardening. These delicious fruit-producing plants include strawberries, blueberries, raspberries, and blackberries.

Strawberries

Generally, all berries are susceptible to insect pests as well as hungry birds. However, if you take this into account when you structure a raised bed for strawberries, for example, you will ensure you have sufficient netting to keep them protected at ground level as well as from above.

Strawberries can be successfully planted through small holes in a sheet of gardening plastic, which is then laid in the raised bed and covered with soil. The plastic sheeting acts as a deterrent to insects that move upwards from the root system and attack the leaves and fruits of the plant.

Strawberries can grow in-ground beds, raised beds, and large containers. Light gauze netting is required to cover the entire raised bed to protect the fruit from flying insects and birds.

To produce that sweet taste, strawberries need to flourish in cold weather. You'll need a lot of sun and some row covers to protect the small plantings from extreme weather. Choose fertile soil without weeds. Place each plant around 18 inches from another. Strawberry patches can produce abundantly from three to four years. They are best harvested in springtime. Pick them in the morning without removing the short, green stub. Wash them in running water before eating or refrigerating.

Strawberries throw out runners that attach into the soil to begin a new plant. These runners can be cut off and replanted in new containers. Thus, a single strawberry plant is sufficient to start with.

Raspberries and Blackberries

Although raspberry and blackberry plants tend to become particularly invasive in a traditional garden, they grow particularly well within the confines of a raised bed where they are easier to control and give a prolific yield.

Bear in mind that if you choose to cultivate these particular berries, the plants will require adequate support for their vines.

Blueberries

Another delicious and much sought-after fruit is the blueberry that grows on a bush. The dwarf variety is perfect for a raised bed garden. Check the best variety for your needs and space (CPC, 2018).

Because blueberries do particularly well in more acidic soil, it is easier to cater to their needs in a smaller, separate raised garden bed. Regular checks on the soil pH will ensure a bumper crop of these tasty, succulent, and healthy fruits.

Cool, Succulent Melons

Certain melon varieties are great for raised beds. Among these are the cantaloupe and honeydew melons. Watermelons may also be a successful choice (CPC, 2018).

Remember, all types of melons need space, as their vines spread for many feet. If you have a sturdy support structure, the smaller varieties may be happy to climb. Melons also require heaps of water, so by keeping these plants well-hydrated, you will ensure an abundant crop.

Take care to manage the vines to avoid them moving in among all your other plants and becoming a tangled mess.

Crunchy Cucumbers

Lindsay Mattison (2019), in her upbeat and informative article, How to Grow Cucumbers: 8 All-Star Tips for Your Best Crop Yet, gives great advice on how to grow these juicy fruits.

Like tomatoes, cucumbers are usually grouped with vegetables. However, these botanically considered fruits are a wonderful asset to any raised bed garden.

These juicy, crunchy fruits thrive in well-ventilated soil, and they enjoy good drainage and the containment style of cultivation in a raised bed garden.

Cucumber cultivars are divided into two distinct types:

- Pickling cucumbers, which are often smaller with rougher, prickly skin, have a short life span.

- Slicing cucumbers are generally larger and juicier than their pickling cousins. They have smooth skin and a longer fruiting period.

You can successfully grow cucumbers from seed. These should be planted in well-draining trays, which will be kept indoors until after the last frost date when they can be transferred to your outdoor raised garden.

Mattison (2019) indicates that within two months of planting, your first cucumbers should be ready for harvesting. These wonderful plants will continue to produce fruit for as long as you keep picking ripe cucumbers off the vines.

Allow the cucumber to reach maturity but take care not to leave them on the vine too long, warns Mattison (2019). Cucumbers that grow too big can become soggy and yellow.

Cucumber vines require warmth and lots of good nutrients as well as compost. Their vines also need to be supported by a sturdy trellis. This will help lift the cucumbers off the soil, thus protecting them from crawling pests. Lifting the cucumbers also encourages better airflow and avoids the development of powdery mildew, says Mattison (2019).

Cucumbers make a great salad and are delicious when served as a chilled soup, which is ideal for hot summer lunches.

Tasty, Tangy Tomatoes

Although tomatoes are often classed as a vegetable, they are, in fact, fruits.

Most tomato varieties thrive in raised beds as they require lots of sunlight to produce prolific quantities of fruit.

Tomato plants grow well in rich, well-drained, acidic soil that has a pH of between 6.5 and 6.8.

To ensure your success in growing these fruits, be reminded that because tomatoes enjoy the warmth, seedlings should only be planted in raised garden beds when the temperature reaches a consistent 60 degrees F, suggests Lucy Mercer (2018) in her informative article, Top Tips for Growing the Best Tomatoes Ever.

Mercer (2018) gives a neat tip for ensuring your tomatoes develop into robust, prolific producers. When transplanting long-stemmed tomato seedlings lay the lower portion of the stem on the soil in the raised bed and cover it with soil. Gently bend the remaining portion upward and secure this area of the stem to a suitably sturdy plant supporter. Because tomato plants shoot roots from the nodes along their stems, these extra roots will secure the plant firmly in the ground.

Tomato plants require lots of good nutrition and water so don't spare the care! Turn in extra compost and keep these 'little gems' well hydrated.

To grow sturdy and upright, tomato plants should be well-supported. Without this, they not only flop into the raised bed, hindering the growth of their fellow plants, but untended tomato plants quickly get out of hand. Decide early on how you plan to support your tomato plants. A cage system may work, or perhaps you may prefer to use individual stakes.

You will also need to regularly cut back all the 'sucker stems,' advises Mercer (2018). This ensures the main plant can focus on fruit production, rather than wasting its resources on side stems.

Zesty Citrus

In her informative article, Growing Citrus in Planters, Cathy Cromwell (n.d.) states you do not have to live in the Sunbelt to grow your citrus. The wide variety of dwarf citrus plants that is available affords most gardeners the chance to cultivate these rewarding plants in their raised bed gardens.

Citrus is not only an attractive evergreen, but the exhilarating and fresh perfume from its delicate flowers will be an asset to your garden. The joy of picking your citrus fruit is a bonus to growing these amazing little plants.

According to Cromwell (n.d.), citrus requires a daily dose of a minimum of eight hours of sunshine. Full-spectrum grow-lights can supplement natural sunlight if your citrus is grown indoors.

Varieties of citrus that do well in raised bed gardens include mandarin, grapefruit, lemon, and orange. Cromwell (n.d.) further indicates these dwarf citrus varieties are susceptible to the cold and should, therefore, be brought indoors during the winter months, where the climate is very cold.

In milder climates, plants can be well-covered with a suitable frost protection cloth such as a Garden-Quilt Cover.

Kumquat and lime are the most resilient citrus capable of withstanding temperatures between 20°F and 32°F.

The Correct Soil Mix

A good-quality inorganic planting mix, specially formulated for planters, will be best for your citrus. The percentage of vermiculite is important, as this will allow for good drainage as well as root aeration.

Mix some larger particles, such as wood or pine chips, into the vermiculite to create more air pockets around the roots.

Fine soil and compost are not recommended for citrus as they tend to compact around the roots, thus stifling them.

The Secret to Successful Planting of Citrus

Cromwell (n.d.) says it is important to locate the 'graft union' on the trunk. Remove any shoots below this point and make sure the 'graft union' remains above soil level when you transplant the citrus plant into your raised bed garden.

Feeding and Fertilizing Citrus

The roots of all containerized plants are forced to remain within the confines of their pot. For this reason, it is essential to offer sufficient water and nutrients to the plant to ensure its continued growth.

However, overwatering will cause root rot. So, a good rule of thumb is to water sufficiently to ensure the water drains out of the bottom of the pot. You should establish a watering routine where you use a moisture soil meter to gauge the level of hydration around the roots. Only water the citrus plant when required.

You may find when the weather is particularly warm; your citrus will require water more frequently.

Citrus are generally 'hungry' plants, requiring regular added feeding. Cromwell (n.d.) suggests a good fertilizer that contains phosphorus, potassium, and nitrogen as well as trace elements such as iron, manganese, zinc, and magnesium.

Blackberries

Blackberries are the type of plants that can bear after your first year of planting. They can continue bearing more for several years even with minimal care. Some types of blackberries are semi-trailing and would need trellis or fences to maintain the upright position. Guide and prune them regularly like you would a rose. You can plant them in either a sunny spot or a semi-shaded spot with good drainage soil. Include a good 3 inches of compost for a year. Planting is best done in early spring or even late winter. In the middle of summer, prune the top not more than 6 inches to trigger growth. Forty days after it has bloomed, your blackberries are ready for harvest. Careful harvesting should be done in the morning while they are still cool. Refrigerate immediately to avoid spoiling.

Cucumbers

Cucumbers are the best choice for those delicious pickles. These plants can be very rewarding to new gardeners for they mature rapidly and are extremely productive. They thrive best in warm weather. Cucumbers can be sown directly into the beds a couple of weeks after the frost of the last spring. When the warm temperature is constant and the soil has enough moisture, cucumber seeds can sprout within just five days. Plant them in the sunniest area with a spacing of about 6 feet. Mix your compost 2 inches deep into the surrounding soil. Harvest them as soon as you see your ideal fruit size. Pick them regularly because cucumbers tend to double their size in a day. Snip them, scrub, pat, and refrigerate to preserve freshness.

Eggplant

Eggplants will flourish during the long summer seasons. You can begin by growing the seeds indoors six weeks before spring. Keep them under fluorescent light for 16 hours while winter is still howling outside. Then transplant them to containers until leaves start to appear. When they reach 8 weeks, you can plant them directly to your soil beds. One plant can produce up to 5 pounds of eggplants in over two months. Loosen the beds before planting them in a sunny spot. Mix in your compost and give them enough water. Provide a 2 feet spacing for each eggplant and prepare some stake for support. When they start bearing fruits, press a firm thumb on the smooth, glossy skin. If it quickly bounces back, then it's harvest time. Prune them while keeping the cap intact. You can store them in a cool room even without refrigeration but no more than a couple of days.

Grapes

Grapes can grow in almost any weather condition but to produce that sweet taste, it needs to thrive in a colder climate. Grape seeds can start indoors four to six weeks before spring. Plant them in the beds in early summer with full sun exposure. Make sure that you dig the soil deep for the water drainage and place about 2 inches of compost. Plant them with a 7 t0 9 feet spacing and place trellis for support. Prune grapes regularly to prevent the growth of the disease. When fruits start maturing from red or white to black or blue, they are ripe and ready for harvest. Snip the cluster and don't wash them. Refrigerate in closed plastic bags.

Melons

Mouthwatering and packed with nutrients, melons are best grown in a warm climate. In humid weather, melons can mature in just 80 to 100 days. They need fertile soil with good drainage and 3 feet spacing. Mix in the 2-inch compost and let them have enough water. You'll know they're ready for harvest because melons tend to slip from their vine when they are ripe. You can easily tug the fruits from the vines. Keep melons at room temperature for 3 hours and not more. Then move them to a refrigerator. This will help bring out all those juicy flavors.

Peppers

Bring some heat into your garden! This striking fruit grows best during the warm summers. Plant these spicy seeds indoors for a week before moving them outside. Pick the spot where the sun is brightest and plant them in a fertile, aerated, and loosen the soil. Combine an inch of compost with the dirt. Water them generously. You can harvest mature peppers in different colors- green, yellow, red, or orange. Snip them from the plant without removing the stub and put them in a freezer.

Goose Berries

Before you consider growing Gooseberries, check and make sure they are legal in your state. Goose Berries are commonly afflicted with White Pine Blister Rust and are forbidden in states where there are many White Pine trees.

If you are permitted to grow one, make sure you have the proper amount of space, these bushes can reach heights of five feet and be just as wide!

Gooseberries are popular in jams, jellies, and preserves. Gooseberries are also used to make tea, as a flavoring for soft drinks, and sometimes made into wine.

There are several different varieties available and all of them taste different, so be sure to do some research first, to find one that you like best.

Plant these in a high sunlight area and use well-drained soil. You should be able to harvest some berries after the second year but waiting until the fourth or fifth year will tend to produce a better-tasting berry.

Gooseberries are a good source of Pantothenic Acid, Vitamin C, and fiber. By the way- no one is sure why they are called "Goose Berries." Geese don't like them.

Apples

An apple tree is a fine addition to just about any backyard able to accommodate one. The best thing to do, if you're interested in your apple tree is to visit a local orchard to see which varieties do well in your area. You may also want to purchase a sapling, since growing a tree from seed will take more time than most would want to wait.

Apples are not native to North America but were brought here in the 1600s by European settlers and the first apple orchard was planted in 1625. Apples have a long history of human use and may have even been the first tree to be cultivated by people thousands and thousands of years ago.

Most people eat apples raw, but they are also good baked and are commonly used in pies and other desserts as well as juices, ciders, and vinegar. Culinary uses for apples are nearly limitless, making them a good choice for a backyard garden.

Apples are a healthy alternative to common snack foods and pack quite a nutritional punch. High in fibers and a decent source of trace minerals, the apple is a solid choice for your garden.

Aside from the fruits and berries mentioned above, the perennial family also contains many useful herbs that are also simple to grow and care for.

Figs

SEED OR PLANT: is planted in autumn or early spring.

CLIMATIC REQUIREMENTS: should be placed in a sunny position and perhaps sheltered by a wall, because it is not very resistant to the cold and can remain outdoors without protection only if the winter temperature is not particularly cold. It loves dry climates and cannot stand humid and foggy areas.

CULTIVATION: the soil must not be too compact but light, well-drained, and slightly calcareous. Irrigation must be regular and administered in such a way that the soil of the pots does not dry out completely.

HARVEST AND USE: the re-flowering varieties ripen in June and August, the others from mid-summer to early autumn depending on the variety. The figs are ready for harvest when they become soft, and their skin cracks.

Citrus

SEED OR PLANT: the citrus plants obtained from seed bear bad fruit; therefore, it is preferable to buy ready and, above all, already grafted, plants, to be transplanted in late spring when the danger of frosts will have passed. The container for an adult plant must measure at least 18 inches in width and depth.

CLIMATIC REQUIREMENTS: citrus fruits prefer warm climate zones and mid-shade exposure, sheltered from strong winds but not light breezes.

Their ideal temperature is between 55 and 86°F (13 and 30°C), therefore in very cold regions, strong winter protection must be provided. The pots can be placed in an unheated but bright room, or, but only if the frosts are not too long, you can wrap the foliage of the plants with a cloth of TNT fabric and wrap the pot with insulating material.

CULTIVATION: They grow well in light, fertile, and rich in organic matter soils (special citrus fruit soils are available on the market). They want abundant and regular watering with non-calcareous water, which in winter will have to be reduced but not completely suspended: citrus fruits do not withstand prolonged drought. However, they fear water stagnation: to avoid it, keep the pots raised from the floor, resting them on a support. Every year, at the beginning of spring, good fertilization with a complete and iron-rich fertilizer is indispensable.

HARVEST AND USE: Citrus Fruits bear fruits from November to March, but some lemon varieties bloom and bear fruits throughout most of the year. The fruits can remain on the plant long enough, even when they are completely ripe. Harvest Citrus Fruits by cutting them off with pruning shears or by pulling them stalk from the tree.

CHOICE GUIDE: citrus fruits are at the top of the list of plants capable of satisfying both the palate and the eyes. Beautiful and decorative for the shiny, evergreen leaves, the intensely scented flowers, and the yellow or orange fruits.

Due to their limited development, the most suitable for cultivation in pots is the Mandarin (Citrus Reticulata), the Calamondino (C. Mitis), a hybrid between Mandarin and Kumquat, and the Lemon (C. Limon) especially in the "Florentia" variety which flowers and bears fruit in every season.

Peach

SEED OR PLANT: the bare-root plants are to be buried in winter, during the vegetative rest period. Potted plants, on the other hand, can be transplanted in February.

CLIMATIC REQUIREMENTS: to be at ease, the Peachtree must live in areas with a fairly harsh winter climate.

CULTIVATION: wants a medium texture soil, fresh but free of water stagnation, while it does not tolerate calcareous soils. Irrigation must be regular during the hot season, and fertilization, to be

90

administered at the end of winter, must be rich in nitrogen and potassium.

HARVEST AND USE: the harvest period is from June to the end of August for the common peaches and from July to August for the nectarines.

CHOICE GUIDE: Only varieties specially selected for the pots can be grown on the terraces.

Apricot

SEED OR PLANT: it is planted during the winter (but not on the coldest days), taking into account that, once adult, the plant will need a pot 18 inches wide and deep.

CLIMATIC REQUIREMENTS: the apricot blossoms quite early, and therefore can be exposed to late frosts. It prefers mild climates, and in any case, where it is protected from cold returns and northern winds. It grows well in dry and little rainy areas, where the risks of cryptogamic diseases are also lesser.

CULTIVATION: it prefers light, warm and permeable soils because its roots cannot stand water stagnation. It should be fertilized at the beginning of the vegetative recovery with a slow-release fertilizer.

HARVEST AND USE: the fruits ripen from the end of May to the end of July, depending on the variety and climate zone.

Chapter 6: Some Common Mistakes with First Time Growers of Fruit Trees

Container gardens tend to have fewer problems than normal gardens because you use clean soil, and it is a closed system. However, you can still encounter issues is to help you avoid some of the common mistakes people make when starting their container garden.

Fill Large Containers in Place

Large containers are very heavy when they are filled with soil so you need to move the empty container to its final position and then fill it. This way you are going to avoid damaging yourself.

Make Large Containers Lighter

If you are planting large containers with shallow-rooted plants then you can fill the bottom third or so of the container with filler material, e.g., empty plastic soda bottles, and then cover it with some plastic screening. This helps make the container lighter as well as reduces the amount of soil required to fill it.

Avoid Overwatering

One of the most common problems people have with a container garden is drainage. All your containers need to have plenty of drainage holes and free-draining soil unless the plant specifically has other requirements. Be careful of using saucers under your containers as these collect water and will need emptying to avoid your plants getting waterlogged. Remember, test the soil with your finger (stick it in up to the second knuckle and see if the soil is dry at your fingertip) before you water. Overwatering can cause the leaves to yellow and drop, also a sign of mineral deficiency, but check the soil isn't too wet before you apply extra fertilizer. Check your plants after heavy rain showers and pour out any excess water pooled in your containers.

Avoid Underwatering

This goes without saying really and you are walking a fine line between watering too much and too little. You will usually need to water once a day as a minimum though on hotter days expect to water twice a day. In hotter climates, an irrigation system can save you a lot of work watering! Soak your plants when you water them until water comes out of the bottom of your pot so that all of the soil is soaked, and the roots can get to the water.

Rescue Dried Out Pots

If your container dries out then put the entire container in a bucket of water and leave it for about 20 to 30 minutes (don't submerge the plant, just the container). This should give the soil enough soaking that the plant can be rescued. For larger pots (which won't fit in a bucket) poke holes in the soil (carefully) with a skewer or stick and then water generously. Wait for about an hour and then water again.

Plant to Pot Ratio

Always consider how your plants look in your container when planting. A large container with lots of small plants will look peculiar and "not right" because the size of the container makes the plants look stunted. If you are planting for aesthetics then you want at least one plant per container that is as tall as your container and to have plants that tumble over the sides to help mask the harsh lines of the pot.

Avoid Damaged, Sickly or Weak Plants

The temptation to get a bargain at your garden store and buy the reduced plants is high and sometimes you can resuscitate them. However, check any plants you buy and make sure they are not damaged or diseased and are in generally good health. The bargain plants can be great, but you can end up with a high mortality rate with them. Damaged plants should be avoided as the damage can often introduce disease into the plant and therefore into your container garden.

Don't Be Scared to Prune

A lot of people are frightened of pruning their plants because they don't want to damage them. Most vegetable plants will not require pruning, but some herbs (lavender and rosemary) and fruit trees will. Other flowers and shrubs can also require regular pruning to keep them looking good. You can save some money by potting on prunes from shrubs using some rooting powder and growing new plants from these cuttings.

Ensure Good Neighbors

Make sure that you group plants with similar requirements for soil, soil, water, and food together in the same containers. Grouping plants together that have different requirements will end up with some dying. You can use double potting to put plants with different requirements in the same container. The plants are potted up in individual containers and then these are put into a larger container.

Feed Your Plants

Remember that your plants require regular feeding as the nutrients in the containers will soon be used up. During winter, you don't need to feed most plants but during spring and the growing season, they will need regular feeding. How often and how much they need feeding will depend on the plant so check out the labels to know how to treat them. A handful of pelleted chicken manure applied in the winter to each pot will help restore much-needed micro-nutrients to the soil.

Don't Be Afraid to Discard a Plant

Plants die. Sometimes from disease, sometimes from the weather and sometimes they just die. Do not be afraid to get rid of a plant if it is looking dreadful, particularly if your container garden is meant to look good. If the plant is diseased then you need to get rid of it as soon as you can to prevent the disease from spreading.

Be Realistic and Plan

Think about your lifestyle when setting up your container garden and plan so that your container plants will thrive. If you travel a lot,

97

particularly in summer then you need to install an irrigation system or use self-watering containers or make good friends with your neighbors!

Grow What You Like

Your container garden is there for you to enjoy so plant what you like in them! If you like tomatoes, grow tomatoes, but if you don't, then don't grow them! Don't feel you have to grow things just because you ought to. If you like flowers then grow those. You can even grow vegetables and plant flowers in the same containers so not only do you get the color from the flowers but the produce from the vegetables. Your container garden is there for you to enjoy therefore you need to plant it with the things you want to grow because you will then be more motivated to look after and care for it.

Don't Put Gravel in the Bottom of a Pot

It is a myth that gravel, pot shards, or stones in the bottom of a container help drainage. It doesn't. These can be useful to ensure the soil doesn't block the drainage holes, but they do nothing to help water drain from your pots and certainly cannot be used instead of drainage holes. All that happens is the roots grow into the gravel in which water pools, so your plants still get waterlogged!

Check Out the Light

Plants need light to grow so you need to be aware of where the sun is in your garden and how it tracks across your containers. Position the sun-loving plants where they get maximum sun and those that like partial shade can go in the areas that get less sun. Remember that plants cast shadows that you can use to your advantage in shading tender plants, but the same shadows can prevent plants from getting enough sun.

Make a List Before You Buy

A shopping list for your container garden is essential when starting. If you don't then you end up buying stuff you don't need and not buying stuff you need. You end up with far too many plants and not enough pots and similar problems. Always make a list of everything you need and then stick to it (easier said than done) when shopping for your container garden to ensure you get everything you need.

Keep Plant Labels

Plant labels contain useful information such as how big your plant will grow, what light it needs, how much food it needs, and more. A lot of gardeners will throw these away not realizing that they can be very useful later when you are either trying to remember what a particular plant is or trying to work out what to plant with it. Keep the labels safe so that you can refer to them when you need to and give your plants the care they need.

Acclimate Your Plants

Plants can take a fair bit of abuse, but they generally don't like sudden changes in weather or light. If you move seedlings outdoors without giving them a chance to get used to it you can end up either with a lot of plants dying or their growth is slowed as they adjust.

Young plants or plants which have spent a lot of time indoors need to be slowly introduced to the outdoors over a couple of weeks. Put them out during the day and bring them in at night and repeat, leaving them out longer into the evening until they are out all night. Remember though if there is any risk of frost to bring them back in again. The process is called hardening off and is vital if you grow from seed.

Troubleshooting for Most Common Problems

No garden is perfect. Like life, you are going to experience problems in container gardening. You will make some mistakes along the way, but do not let this stop you from enjoying your garden. You will probably ask yourself what you did wrong that your vegetable plants have dry leaves, or brittle stems even when you were very careful in watering or fertilizing the plants. Do not worry. The chances are that these problems were caused by outside factors such as unpredictable weather, and/or temperature.

Listed below are common problems and concerns in container gardening:

1. My plants are wilting, even when watered frequently. What should I do?

   - There is a lack of oxygen due to insufficient drainage and aeration.

   - Too much water because drainage problems block the oxygen's access to the roots.

2. Check the drainage holes of your container, and unblock if clogged, or increase the number of drainage holes.

   - Use a growth medium that is porous, or more lightweight.

3. My plants look small, purple, and stopped growing. What happened?

   - Conditions were too cold.

   - They are not receiving enough sunlight.

   - Relocate the plants to an area with ample sunlight, and a warmer temperature. Chances are, cold temperature or cool conditions do not work well with your plants, thus, preventing the plant from growing because it cannot take up phosphorus from the soil.

4. The leaves and branches of a healthy plant droop once they are watered. Why did this happen?

- They have an insufficient drainage structure.

- Check the drainage holes of the container. Excess water blocks oxygen from entering the roots and soil.

5. The leaves or fruits of my plants have holes and irregular shapes. How do I fix this?

   - They are damaged by insects and pests such as leaf miners, worms, or bugs.

   - Remove the insects and pests by using insecticides. Be careful in choosing the type of insecticide that you will use.

6. I noticed that some leaves have white mold on them. What does this mean?

   - They have a fungal disease.

   - The weather is too cold/damp.

   - This is a fungal disease called 'Powdery Mildew' that is common to plants affected by cold, or damp weather. Relocate the plants to an area with ample sunlight and a warmer temperature. Remove and discard the affected leaves.

Aside from the solutions to these common gardening problems, here are some additional tips:

1. Clean the containers thoroughly before using them. This will kill any pests and remove leftover fertilizer salts.

2. Some plants are very sensitive to cold weather, requiring protection from the wind and the cold such as mulching, windscreens, or relocating to a warmer area.

3. When planting vining plants, secure them to stakes, poles, cages, or other support structures to prevent the plants from bending, or blowing over.

4. Elevate your containers using bricks, or wood blocks, and place a saucer, or a small pot to catch the drained water. Change and clean regularly to prevent mosquitoes from breeding in the water.

Chapter 7: Useful Tips

Determine Your Growing Zone

Knowing your growing zone will help you understand your general growing climate and which plants will likely thrive there. Divided into 11 categories, growing zones are calculated based on the average annual minimum temperature in each location.

Growing zones were created to help gardeners understand which perennial plants will survive the winter in a particular location. Because annual plants complete their life cycle in one season and do not survive the winter, growing zones technically do not apply to them.

Although your zone won't matter for most vegetables and herbs you grow, knowing it can help you understand which plants grow best in certain seasons, which plant varieties may grow better, and which plants may not grow at all.

For example, gardeners in cooler zones 1 to 4 might grow cool-weather crops all summer, but their season isn't long enough to support heat-loving crops such as okra and large melons. Gardeners in warmer zones 7 to 11 usually can't grow cool-weather crops such as lettuce in the summer, but they can grow them in fall and winter.

Seed packets, seed catalogs, and plant tags are great resources. They specify if a plant can grow in your zone.

Identifying Microclimates

In addition to knowing your growing zone, it's important to consider factors unique to your yard. The nuances of your specific location, or microclimate, alter your growing conditions and can also affect when you get frosts. Frost dates are key to knowing when and what to plant.

Microclimates can occur around structures, mountains, bodies of water, slopes, and more. Gardens planted next to a south-facing wall, for example, may have higher heat that prevents tomato fruit from forming in warmer zones, but creates a greater yield of peppers in cooler zones.

Gardens in the shadow of a mountain, in a valley, or at the bottom of a slope may get frosts later in the spring and earlier in the fall than surrounding higher elevations. This type of microclimate may require a gardener to delay summer planting or to cover frost-prone plants.

These are just a few examples of microclimate variations, and you should pay attention to how your plants respond to your microclimate. Make a note of your area's average last- and first frost dates and compare them to what you experience from year to year. If your conditions vary from what is considered average for your area, you can adjust your crops and the timing of your plantings accordingly.

Consider Your Garden Type and Space

Most plants are happy to grow in containers, raised beds, or the ground. However, some are better suited to one form or another.

Some herbs (e.g., mint, lemon balm, and oregano) spread aggressively, which makes them ideal for a container. If you plant them in a raised or in-ground bed, they will take over and smother other plants.

Some crops are considered "heavy feeders," which means they need more nutrients than others. Therefore, although heavy feeders such as tomatoes, squash, cabbage, and broccoli grow well in containers, they enjoy the moisture-holding capacity of raised beds, and the greater access to soil nutrients reduces the need for regular supplemental fertilizer.

Raised beds are also ideal for crops that require more plants for a plentiful harvest, such as beans, peas, and okra.

Some plants also need more space than others. If you're looking to maximize the yield of your garden, a container full of greens that can feed you for months may be a better choice than a container with one cabbage plant that will give you one head. Pick Plants That Get Along

Vegetables and herbs benefit from companion planting. Scientific research on the topic remains scarce, but we do know that the more diverse your vegetables, herbs, and flowers are, the healthier your garden will be. Some plants do seem to offer a measure of pest control to nearby plants. For example, icicle radishes may repel squash bugs and cucumber beetles. Conversely, some plants negatively affect others when planted nearby. Broccoli and tomatoes, for example, both high uptake levels of calcium. Planting them together could result in smaller broccoli heads and blossom-end rot in tomatoes.

Also, beware that plants in the same families (e.g., cabbage and cauliflower) often are visited by the same pests, are afflicted by the same diseases, and take up similar nutrients from the soil. (Plants that share similar characteristics, such as appearance, general growth habits, and seed and seedling presentation, are grouped into plant families.) In addition to pest control and nutrient needs, there are other benefits to companion planting. Vegetables with varying growth habits and nutrient needs benefit each other (such as planting cooler-weather crops in the shade of heat-loving ones). This is also an excellent way to maximize a small space.

Although some companion planting combinations may benefit your garden, don't dive too deeply into it now. Start with these suggestions and experiment with other combinations later.

Garden Maintenance

Watering as needed. The following guidelines are just that—guidelines. It all comes down to a matter of common sense and paying attention to your plants. If the ground is hot and dry, the plants are going to look parched. Don't leave them like this for very long. Going from one extreme to another is hard on a plant. It stresses their system and affects their ability to perform at maximum capacity.

- Plants that are in the ground usually require the least amount of watering. Unless you are experiencing a drought or excessive heat, most flowers will do just fine with watering two or three times a week. Again, this depends on the amount of rainfall you have, the temperature, and the type of flowers you are growing.

- Some vegetables will require more water if there are little rainfall and high heat. Cucumbers, for example, need a lot more moisture than potatoes and onions.

- Flowers and vegetables in raised beds can usually be watered with the same frequency as in-ground flowers and vegetables.

- Container plants need water much more frequently. They can only hold so much at a time without becoming too wet, so you should never drench a plant in a pot. Water it until the soil is moist and stops. Unglazed ceramic pots are especially thirsty, as their porous composition soaks up the water—even wicking it away from the soil, where it is most needed.

Weeding is one of those things you must do whether you want to or not. One of the best ways to reduce the amount of weeding you will have to do is to start with ground that is as weed-free as possible. Taking the time to get as many weeds as possible out of the ground where your garden area will be is the best thing you can do for yourself and your plants. Aside from that, by spending a few minutes every other day weeding a few rows in the vegetable garden and a few minutes pulling weeds from your flower beds, the task will never seem overwhelming.

Other ways you can cut down on the amount of weeding necessary include using ground cover under your flower beds and covering the surface with rock or mulch, laying ground cover between the rows of your vegetable garden, filling your beds with flowers, and planting something in nearly every inch of available soil in your vegetable garden. NOTE: The motive behind planting things so close together is to reduce the number of spaces weeds can grow.

Some weddings will have to be done by hand—literally pulling the weeds from the ground with your hands. In larger spaces, you can hoe up the dirt all around the plants and then pick the loose weeds out and discard them.

Deadheading is essential for a pretty flower bed. You should get rid of wilted, dried-up blooms daily. This will allow more nutrients from the plant to be used to make more blooms and healthier foliage. To deadhead, simply pull the dead flowers off the plant with your fingers or snip them off with a pair of garden scissors.

Spraying and fertilizing is another 'must.' Spraying for pests can be done periodically just for safety's sake but is usually only done at the first sign of trouble. By keeping this aspect of garden maintenance to a minimum, you will be allowing nature to do its thing, i.e., letting the good bugs take care of the bad ones. There are exceptions, however, to this rule.

For those of you who are anti-chemical, you can use gentler concoctions such as the dish soap spray I've mentioned a few times. Cayenne pepper and water are effective in killing ants, orange oil mixed with water and dish soap kills slugs and roaches, and tobacco and water sprayed on plants kill aphids.

Fertilizing is something you can do for the soil and your plants. You should fertilize the soil every fall and spring by adding compost, manure, or commercial fertilizers to it. Fertilizing plants should be done carefully—not too often and not too heavily. Too much fertilizer 'burns' plants, meaning it is too strong. Over-fertilizing can weaken and even kill a plant.

If your soil is well-fertilized, you won't need to fertilize your plants—especially if they are in the ground or raised beds. Plants raised in pots, straw bales, or hydroponic gardens will need fertilizer. Liquid fertilizers or fertilizer sticks you bury in the soil are your best options. Just be sure to follow the directions on the package. Or, if you prefer to go a more natural route, you can do any of the following:

- Water your plants with fish emulsion mixed with water.

- Spread coffee grounds and finely crushed eggshells on the soil and mix them into the surface of the soil.

- Bury chopped banana peels in your potted plants.

- Water your plants with pure molasses water (1 tablespoon to a gallon of water), unsweet tea, or Epsom salts water (1 tablespoon to a gallon of water).

Caring for your garden is not all that difficult or time-consuming. Unless you have large areas to care for, the average person can do all that needs to be done in the same amount of time it takes to watch one or two television shows. And it's better to tend to potatoes than to be a lazy person.

List of Common Garden Weeds:

- Dandelion

- Purslane

- Plantain

- Quack Grass

- Crab Grass

- Saw Thistle

- Carpet Weed

- Chicken Weed

Keeping Pests Away from The Container Garden

You have started a container garden; your fruits and vegetables are thriving and along comes a pest. It may be the four-legged version or the slimy, creepy crawlies. There are ways to protect and keep your fruits and vegetables from being destroyed.

Now most gardeners have opted to be chemical-free, but if not, there are plenty of pesticides and insecticides to keep your plants safe. If you like chemical-free, there are plenty of options to prevent those pests from eating your produce and demolishing your fruits and vegetables, which you have spent time and money cultivating.

As a gardener beginner, you will want to look at your plants and examine what is eating them. Remember that ninety percent of insects are beneficial, and we do not want to kill these as they eat the ones who destroy our plants. When using pesticides, keep in mind that all insects both the good and the bad will be killed, throwing off the garden's ecosystem.

The easiest pests to get rid of are snails and slugs. They eat the leaves and leave nice holes in your produce.

The cheapest route is to take an orange and or grapefruit half that is used and place grape juice or beer into them. These slimy creatures can't resist these smells and taste and will delve in.

In the morning, you can pick up the fruit half and snails/ slugs and dispose in the trash or kill your pest and throw it in the compost heap.

If you do not have fruit halves, fill a saucer with the beer or grape juice, mixed with a teaspoon of salt, and these lovelies will dive right in and drown. If this is too much for those of you who love critters, it is said that copper wire or copper taping placed around your pots will keep these creatures at bay.

After some, there is some maintenance required for this to work. The copper must stay clean, and no grass or leaves, or branches can rest or grow up against the pots as the snails/slugs will be able to crawl up into your containers. Then there is the old-fashioned way of just picking them off and moving them to another location.

The one good thing about growing your fruits and vegetables in containers is that you can inspect them daily. Hence you can remove any tomato worms, caterpillars, or any other destructive insect that you may see, leaving behind the ladybugs and praying mantis to do their job.

Organic sprays have also come along way. Several good varieties are Rose Farm, peppermint spray, which smells wonderful but keeps insects at bay, 100% garlic oil, which is sprayed on the leaves that are being chewed, preventing further damage.

There are insect soaps that are sprayed on the bugs, making them vulnerable to their surroundings. If spraying, picking, and examining your plants is too much work, there is a row cover that is lightweight that can be placed over your plants, allowing air, light, and water to come through but protects your plants from pests.

Unfortunately, this takes away from the aesthetics of garden containers, but they could be used at night, allowing your plants to be protected from evening pests.

The most common complaint in gardening is squirrels and chipmunks; these cute critters will demolish flower bulbs in minutes, eat your greens, and just ruin your mood for gardening. The easiest route is to place wire mesh over your containers before they have sprouted up.

Make sure to secure firmly as these pests are extremely intelligent. River rock and larger gravel also seem to keep them out of containers, and it gives your containers a very natural and pleasing appeal. Like other animals, squirrels and chipmunks do not like strong odors.

Coffee grounds are a great deterrent and are found in almost everyone's home. The grounds can be mixed in with your soil, or spread around the parameters of your container garden. Coffee is also high in acidity, so it is extremely good for most of your garden plants. Soap bars are another great way to keep four-legged pests away. Tied on a string or laying around containers will deter.

Try another smelly deterrent that will make rabbits, skunks, squirrels, and deer stay away. Fox and coyote urine will deter most mammals as they fear that a predator is lurking in the area.

This spray can last you all season and keep the pest at large. Reflective tape, anything that moves or makes noise will also help with annoying animals and send them scurrying into your neighbor's yard or up the street.

Another easy solution is to place a birdbath near your containers, the bath will attract birds and keep bugs at bay. This lovely addition will also give you complete happiness as you get to see a variety of birds come around.

Plant flowers that will draw in the good bugs, such as bees and butterflies, to pollinate your containers, along with the flowers. Plant herbs that will distract the bad bugs from eating your treasures.

Conclusion

Thank you for making it to the end!

Having read this book, hopefully, you have gained a much greater insight into all aspects of fruit gardening. For those who truly enjoy the hobby, it is very much an art form and is something that is relaxing and inspiring. Hobby gardening is practiced across the world by people of many different cultures, and fruit gardening has been a great way to open that practice up to people in urban environments, renters, and people who reside in areas with no fertile soil.

Hobby fruit gardening is also remarkably popular with children, the elderly, and the disabled, as it gives people a chance to explore their creative sides and to nurture and care for another living thing, and to watch it thrive.

Fruit gardening is a great way to show off your artistic skills. Many people find themselves with a few creative outlets when trying to juggle a career and a family.

For many of these people, the simple act of growing plants and caring for them can be a great way to release frustration and express their natural creative abilities. Creating elaborate arrangements and putting them out for the entire world to see can be remarkably beneficial.

In addition to benefits such as expression and edible plants, there are many health benefits to fruit gardening as well. The act of caring for and tending plants can go a long way towards fighting anxiety and depression for many people. It encourages the mind and body to slow down and to appreciate the small things that surround us. It is excellent for people of all ages and can have a significant impact on both physical and emotional health.

When it comes to kids and teenagers, gardening is great for teaching lessons about earning rewards. When a young person is taught through experience that by giving to these plants every day, they can be rewarded with fresh fruits and vegetables that can provide them and their community with nutrition. Gardening can also help them to foster a healthy respect for nature and the environment as well as a healthy attitude towards learning.

For elderly individuals, gardening offers many physical and emotional benefits. In addition to benefits such as lowering depression rates, gardening helps to eliminate boredom and loneliness by providing a rewarding activity that can be easy to do. Physical benefits of fruit gardening include improved dexterity and hand strength, as well as improved coordination and eye strength. For people who exhibit low physical activity, the exercise provided by moderate gardening can be enough to help improve or maintain health. Many health institutions have recognized these benefits, and gardening programs are becoming more common in senior living communities as well as gaining more recommendations from general physicians.

Another benefit of fruit gardening is that it can be an excellent source of food or herbs. Many people grow vegetables, fruits, and herbs in containers both inside and outside of their homes. When you create a successful garden, you will likely be surprised to find how few plants it takes to provide your family with the vegetables, herbs, and fruits needed to sustain you through the growing season. Many people choose to cultivate extra plants so that they can or jar fruits and vegetables or dry herbs for use during winter.

Still, others choose to use fruit gardening to brighten and beautify their homes and property. There are endless ways to use plants to freshen a space and to add color and flair. Whether lining a driveway, creating a flower bed or covering the foundation of your home, there is much you can do to use fruit gardens to enhance the outside of your home. Many people create elaborate landscaping designs using only container plants. With an eye for color, an understanding of what plants will thrive best in your area, and a knack for picking the right containers for each plant and space, you can certainly achieve a yard or area that looks as though it was designed by professionals while spending only a modest amount of time and money.

The benefits you see with your fruit garden will mostly be determined by your expectations. If you step into this project or hobby, expecting to put your plants outside and watch as they continue to flower and bloom, you are likely to experience disappointment. If, on the other hand, you expect to invest time and effort feeding, watering, pruning, and caring for your plants, you are apt to find yourself quite satisfied. Plants are much like people in that they must be nurtured to thrive.

No matter what your age, there is much to be gained through gardening. This hobby offers an array of physical and emotional health benefits and can provide a great way to boost self-esteem while lowering rates of depression and suicide. Caring for plants can be a great way to give back to the world around you while enjoying an activity that is relaxing and cathartic. Whether you are seeking a way to alleviate stress or a chance to enjoy the fresh air before work, tending container plants offers an ideal solution.

In all, the benefits of fruit gardening are simply immeasurable. Whether you are seeking to implement a few hanging garden baskets in your home or on your porch or are seeking to create a beautifully landscaped front yard, you will find that gardening is simply good for you.

Learning to master fruit gardening is something that takes a lifetime but learning to enjoy and reap the benefits can be done quickly.

Indoor fruit gardens can be just as rewarding. Whether you are experimenting with organic fruit gardening to create fresh herbs or simply beautifying the rooms in your home, you will find that there are many choices available inside your home. Window boxes and displays can make every room brighter, and a simple plant hanging in a hallway or bathroom can add a splash of life to notoriously drab spaces. With a bit of flair and the right plants, you can draw the eye to the parts of your home that you feel go unnoticed, ensuring that every room of your home is inviting and welcoming to all who enter.

No matter your reason for creating a fruit garden, you will find the hobby quite rewarding, provided, you can invest the time and care needed to develop healthy and thriving plants. This book was designed to help make creating a fruit garden more fun and more rewarding. You will quickly learn that fruit gardening is a great way to get fast and easy results. While maintaining plants requires a bit of work, the effect of placing beautiful arrangements in your home or yard is immediate.

Unlike cultivating an outdoor garden, you will also find that fruit gardening can be perfect for people of all skill levels.

Even if you have never been able to keep a standard houseplant thriving, following the tips and guidelines you have learned within these pages can help you develop a green thumb. Choosing plants that have low care requirements is always great for beginners, and in no time, you will be able to grow beautiful bulbs and flowers with the greatest of ease.

As with any hobby or undertaking, one of the secrets of fruit gardening is to be patient with yourself and your garden. No matter how much effort you put forth, plants will bloom only when in season. Take the time to appreciate new growth and celebrate small accomplishments. When you can care for your plants throughout the year and take the time to prune and deadhead them as needed, you will certainly be rewarded with a bright and long blooming season.

It is important to remember that mistakes and setbacks can happen as well. If you overwater or over-fertilize a plant, take the experience and learn from it. You will not always be a perfect gardener but understanding that even the most advanced gardeners make mistakes will help you move beyond these situations. The needs of your plants can change with shifts in weather, temperature, and climate, and only with experience can you learn how to anticipate what changes you will need to make in caring for them.

You will also need to remember that some seasons will simply be better than others in terms of outdoor fruit gardens. When there has been an extremely hot and dry summer, you can expect to have a harder time maintaining your plants. In many areas, this type of season can spell certain death for all but the hardiest of plants. Don't let rainy or hot seasons and the changes they bring discourage you from gardening. Nature is always going to be difficult to predict, but the benefits of gardening are quite rewarding. If your plants do not survive a particularly hard winter, simply create a new garden and start over. Using more insulation or learning what you can do to prevent the problem is always much better than simply giving up.

As climates change and new plants grow in popularity, there is always something new to be learned in the art of gardening, ensuring that even the professionals will always have more to understand. With the tips and tricks, you have learned in these pages, however, you are certainly well equipped to begin a fruit garden of your own. As with any hobby, the most important things to keep in mind are simple to be creative, take your time, and have fun.

VEGETABLE GARDENING FOR BEGINNERS

THE BEST TECHNIQUES AND SECRETS TO EASILY GROW VEGETABLES AT HOME

Bradley Gray

Introduction

Vegetables are good for you, good for the planet, and tasty, too.

Growing your own vegetables can be very rewarding and is a rewarding skill for your children to learn. A kitchen garden is also a great way of reducing your food bill.

As someone who came from an agricultural family, I am passionate about the benefits of gardening and know that it will be a life skill that your children will always be proud of.

I like to grow most veg in containers at home for ease and this reduces gardening maintenance while still allowing the chance for great harvests.

Vegetables are best grown in a sunny spot in the garden, as they love sunshine and warmth, or in containers close to your kitchen door so you can use them more regularly.

In this book, I'll show you how to grow your own tasty vegetables.

I want you to know that you can also grow your own vegetables even if you have a small space and not a lot of money to invest.

There's really no reason for you not to grow your own vegetables!

Saving money on your food bill and raising your self-sufficiency levels are just two of the benefits of growing your own food.

Vegetables make a great hobby whatever you want to do. - If you an interested in making money from growing then this book shows you how to build up organic vegetables to sell at the market or join the local community growing scheme. - If you just want to grow for personal satisfaction or, if you are keen to teach the children about how things grow and that healthy food comes from the land, then this is also a rewarding hobby.

For those who already have a garden at home, but don't have any real experience of either gardening or growing, cottage gardens are a good option as they are reasonably easy to maintain.

If you have children but your garden is too big for you to look after effectively then container gardening should be a better option for you as it allows you more control over space and soil preparation.

Vegetables grow in all sorts of weather and soil types so everyone can get involved in growing fresh organic produce.

Growing parsley from seeds is one of the easiest things you could possibly do, there is no need to buy seedlings, just simply gather some seeds from the parsley you have been eating and plant them in a sunny spot outside or in a greenhouse. You could also start some indoors on a windowsill if you are short of time or want to be sure that you have fresh parsley all year round.

Growing vegetables on your own might be difficult in the beginning but don't worry, this book will guide you through the process.

If you are just starting out then feel free to start with the easiest vegetable that is also cost-effective at the same time – garlic, after all, it's so easy to grow and

it grows well in containers.

For those who have some experience of gardening already, then there are many other wonderful methods of growing vegetables besides container gardening such as in a greenhouse or even outside in just a small garden patch.

Let us begin.

Chapter 1: Where To Start?

Clearing Your Garden Spot

The first step is cleaning up space so the soil will not be hard to work on. One can clear your garden space any time of the year, but the most optimal is the season before you plant.

1. Outlining the spaces of your garden plot where clearing is needed.

Outlining the areas depend on how you want the plots to be shaped. Try to follow these straightforward guidelines:

If you want the edges of a rectangular or square plot straight, stretch a cord in between the marked line and sticks with white limestone that is ground, which is easily accessible at garden stores.

If you are seeking a circular garden, utilize a rope or hose to outline the area, and ensure that you are fixing the stature to create a leveled curve.

2. Start by clearing the surface. To do this, you will be razing the plants, bushes, weeds, and rocks. Use a mower if you want to cut the weeds and grass near the surface.
3. Dig out the roots of tough weeds and small trees using a hoe, shovel, or pickaxe.

Killing Weeds and Aggressive Grasses

Weeds are the bane of beautiful gardens. Even when you have cultivated a proper garden, you need must weed it from time to time. Be that as it may, weeding is especially important when you are preparing your garden for the first time.

When preparing a garden, you must get rid of the grass and the weeds as much as possible. Depending on the size of the garden, this process can take quite some time to complete.

You can eliminate weeds and active grasses using two ways described below:

Sifting and Digging by hand: In the case of a minute garden digging up the entire earth and cautiously sifting the soil must be done. Carefully remove root and sod parts that might grow up the following year as weeds.

Put a Covering: An easy and chemical-free technique to clear your garden is to cover it with cardboard, clear or black plastic, even old rugs. The existing plants cannot stand these drastic conditions, such as lacking light from the sun and energy, so they eventually die after a month or so.

The plastic rolls can be bought from the home improvement centers and hardware stores. It is necessary that you use the thickest cardboard or plastic. Controlling weeds and grasses by applying covering to your garden spot is straightforward if you follow these steps:

Spread the covering over your entire garden spot, safeguarding the edges with auxiliary rocks, boards, or bricks.

After a month, remove the covers and cut off any grass or weeds with the aid of a shovel. Try to cut at the root level (just underneath the soil surface). If they aren't too thick, a rototiller can be employed.

Analyzing and Improving Your Soil

After you have cleared your garden, the next major step is to have a close look at your soil; give it a hard squeeze, have it checked and tested, improve it, and then work it out to ensure that it is in good shape. Healthy soil gives vegetable roots a balance of all the things they require viz. moisture, air, and nutrients. If you know your soil type, it enables you to neutralize problems that you may face when working on your piece of land.

Testing your soil

Vegetables are kind of fussy about soil chemistry. Excess of a particular nutrient or lack of a particular nutrient, and you have complications.

The quality of the soil is pivotal to the health of the plants. While testing the soil, you need to check for its pH value and make the necessary amendments. You also need to check the drainage of your soil. To do so, you should soak the soil by hosing it down. Let the area remain undisturbed for a day. The next day, take a handful of the soil and squeeze it hard. If you find that water is streaming out of your hand, it means that the drainage of the soil is poor. You should add organic matter or compost for better drainage. Alternatively, you may want to invest in raised beds.

Now, you should check the soil by opening your hand. If you find that the soil has not balled up or the ball breaks down at the slightest touch, the soil may be too sandy. On the other hand, the ball may not break down even if it is poked hard. This denotes that the clay content is high. In both of these cases, you should be adding organic matter. This will improve the texture of the soil and make it suitable for the growth of the plants.

If the ball breaks down when poked, the conditions of the soil are just perfect for plant growth. This is the property of loam soil.

The exact pH enables vegetables to utilize nutrients from the soil. If your soil's pH is not within the specified range, plants can take up the nutrients such as phosphorus and potassium even if they are abundant in the soil. On the other hand, the solubility of certain minerals like manganese may increase to toxic levels if the pH is extremely low.

Most vegetables prefer a slightly acidic environment (pH ranging between 6 and 7) for their optimal growth.

The only way to assess whether your soil is fit for your vegetables is to test it. Don't panic, analyzing your soil is not complex. Here are the two methods to test your soil:

Use a do-it-yourself kit: If you want to access the acidity or alkalinity of your soil, the basic pH test kit can be utilized, available at a nursery. This kit can sometimes assist in calculating the major nutrient content. However, the test only gives you a rough estimate of the pH and nutrient levels in your soil.

Contact a soil lab to do a test for you: A comprehensive soil test might turn out to be a good investment as a soil lab can thoroughly examine your soil. Soil labs don't charge you a lot. Your local Cooperative Extension Service office or private lab can conduct a comprehensive and reliable soil test. It gives you further insight into your soil; here is what you will know in addition to the pH level:

Since we have seen how to analyze the soil, we will now turn our attention to ways of improving the soil.

To grow plants properly, you need to ensure that the soil is the right one for them. Most plants need the soil of neutral pH, but some tend to require alkaline or acidic soils. Whatever be the type of soil you have; it is possible to modify it so that it becomes more suitable for the plant you wish to grow. However, the steps you take will not have an everlasting effect. Unless you are planning to undertake the steps regularly, you should try using the soil that you have.

Adjusting soil pH

To increase the alkalinity of the soil, you can add ground lime. For increasing the acidity, you can use Sulphur or aluminum Sulphate. All Cooperative Extension Service offices, various lawn and garden centers, and many soil labs have charts showing the quantity of lime and sulfur to be added to fix the pH imbalance. You first have to measure the area of your vegetable garden; the chart tells you the quantity in pounds to be added per 1,000 square feet.

Increasing the Soil's Nutrient Content

If you discover that your soil has a low amount of nutrients, you should add some organic matter to it. Manure and compost can enrich the soil while improving its texture. You can also use organic mulches such as deciduous leaves, straw, and dried grass clippings. These mulches can break down and provide the soil with organic nutrients and improve the soil structure at the same time.

Perfect loam soil is rare, so don't worry if you are deprived of it. To fix your grimy clay or loose sand, you need to add organic matter. You can't change your type of soil altogether, but supplementing organic matter makes your soil more like loam, which is impeccable for vegetable roots. Even if you are lucky enough to have loam soil, adding organic matter to your soil every year will further increase productivity.

Organic matter improves the garden soil as it assists loosening and provides proper ventilation to clay soil. It enhances the water and nutrient-holding capacity of sandy soil.

Organic matter attracts vital microorganisms, beneficial fungi, worms, and other soil-borne organisms that enhance the health of your vegetables.

Mulching

The importance of mulching should never be underestimated. It can insulate the soil and thereby keep the roots of plants safe from extremes in temperature. It can also enable the roots to remain moist by retaining water. More importantly, mulching can curb the growth of weeds in your garden.

Various kinds of mulch can be used. You can purchase a range of them at stores. Some of them are specially created to solve certain specific issues in a garden. However, for general purposes, you can easily make mulch at home.

You simply need to gather all dead organic matter in your gardens, such as dead leaves and broken branches. Your garden itself will yield enough plant matter for use as mulch. Collect this organic matter throughout the year in a designated area and break them down into small particles with machines or by hand. Let the mulch remain all winter. The following spring, you will have enough mulch for use in your garden.

Composting

Compost is regarded as the best organic material to supplement your soil. Composting simply breaks down the waste material into a brittle soil-like material called humus. It is easily accessible and pretty straightforward to use.

Compost is basically decayed organic matter. It acts as a natural fertilizer for your garden. It can be an excellent addition to all kinds of soils. You can easily purchase compost at a low cost, even in bulk amounts. On the other hand, you can make your own compost at home for the garden.

There are many other organic matters such as sawdust and manure that can be employed, but compost has surpassed all these organic matters. Using other organic matters except compost can cause problems. For instance, sawdust undoubtedly adds value to your soil upon converting into humus, but when it decomposes, it deprives the soil of nitrogen. It gives rise to the problem of adding more fertilizer to compensate for the effect. In case you are using livestock mature, it will replenish the nitrogen level of the soil, but the abnormal growth of weeds can be observed as livestock diet consists of abundant hay that contains plenty of weed seeds.

It is always good to use fully composted organic matter; that is prepared for a year or two, so it is decomposed completely, and the salts are drained off properly. Too much salt in the soil can be detrimental to plants. Good quality compost and completely decomposed manure should have a dark brown appearance, earthy odor, and have minute original material evident.

Essential Tools For Vegetable Gardening

Many of all the things that you need are likely already around your home -- particularly if you're working on other outside jobs. Here's a brief list of some helpful vegetable gardening equipment:

✓ Gloves allow you to grasp resources better and help you avert hand blisters. Cotton gloves would be the most affordable, but the expensive creature gloves -- made of sheep and goat skin -- last longer.

✓ An excellent straw hat with venting prevents the sunshine from your skin and allows air to move through and cool your mind.

✓ An excellent pocketknife or set of pruning shears is excellent for cutting edge strings and blossoms.

✓ Sturdy rubber boots, garden clogs, or function boots repel water and supply aid for digging.

✓ Bug repellent and sunscreen keep you comfy and secure while working in the garden.

Freezing, Drying, and Canning Veggies

You can conserve vegetables in three distinct ways -- by drying, freezing, or canning them to help your crop last more than if you saved your veggies fresh. I really don't have enough room to explain all the details about these different procedures, however, the following list provides you a thumbnail sketch of each method:

✓ **Freezing:** This is likely the simplest way to conserve vegetables. But if you would like, simply puree up some berries, place them in a container, and toss them in the freezer and they'll last for 4 weeks. The mixture is very good to use in skillet or soups. Blanching is the practice of dunking the vegetables in boiling water for a moment or 2 and then putting them into ice water to cool them off. You then wash the veggies with a towel and then suspend them in labeled plastic freezer bags. Straightforward.

✓ **Drying:** This technique could be rather simple, but it has to be performed correctly to avoid spoilage. Essentially, you dehydrate the veggies by placing them out from the sun to dry, by slow baking them in the oven, or using a commercial dehydrator, which you can purchase in most mail-order catalogs (see the appendix). In hot, sunny climates such as California, you are able to dry 'Roma' tomatoes by slicing them in half and placing them out in sunlight onto a display. Spoilage is obviously an issue, therefore before drying out your veggies, you might have to find some extra info. You usually will need to keep dried veggies in airtight containers; lidded jars work well. You may use dried veggies to create soups and sauces.

✓ **Canning:** Of preserved vegetables, I enjoy the flavor of canned berries the ideal. Nothing tastes better in the midst of winter. But canning is a fragile and labor-intensive process that could require paring, sterilizing jars, cooking, boiling, and also lots of additional work. I typically put aside an entire weekend can tomato and other veggies. I really don't wish to dissuade you, but you want some great recipes, some particular gear, and likely some assistance if you would like to can vegetables.

Placing Off Your Vegetables

You have two options when you harvest your plants: Eat the veggies straight away or keep them to use afterward. Particular veggies need different storage requirements to preserve their freshness. These states can be outlined as follows:

✓ **Cool and dry:** Ideally, temperatures must be between 50° and 60°Fahrenheit, with 60% relative humidity -- states that you usually find at a two-bedroom cellar.

✓ **Cold and dry:** Temperatures must be between 32° and 40°, together with 65% humidity. You may attain these requirements in many home refrigerators or in a cold basement or garage.

✓ **Cool and moist:** Temperatures must be between 50° and 60° with 90% humidity. You're able to store vegetables in a trendy kitchen or cellar in perforated plastic bags.

✓ **Cold and moist:** Ideally, your storage space needs to be 32° to 40°, together with 95% humidity. You are able to make these requirements by putting your veggies in refrigerated bags (veggies in luggage without venting are very likely to hamper quicker) and keeping the bags in a fridge.

Watering Hoses and Cans

Plants need water to grow, and when Mother Nature is not cooperating, you want to water frequently. For a huge garden, you might require fancy soaker hoses, sprinklers, and drip irrigation pipes. However, for many small house gardeners, a very simple hose and watering can perform. Rubber hoses are a lesser chance to kink than nylon or plastic pads, but they are normally much heavier to maneuver around. Whatever material you choose, make sure you acquire a hose that is long enough to reach plants in every area of your garden without needing to take water around the beds to reach far-off plants. Decide on a hose that includes brass fittings and a washer incorporated into the hose; those components make the hose not as likely to fail after prolonged usage. Watering cans can be made from easy, cheap, brightly colored plastic or high-end, fancy metal. Vinyl is lighter, but galvanized metal is rustproof and much more appealing. Watering cans come in various sizes, so try several out for relaxation before purchasing. Ensure it is simple to eliminate the sprinkler head, or improved, for cleanup.

Hand Trowels

Hand Trowels are crucial for digging in containers, window boxes, and little raised beds. The wider-bladed hand trowels that can be brightly shaped and round the conclusion, are simpler to use to loosen dirt compared to narrower bladed, V-pointed ones, these thinner blades are better for grinding tough weeds, like dandelions.

Hand Cultivators

A three-pronged hand cultivator is a useful tool to split up dirt clods, straightforward seedbeds, and also operate in granular fertilizer. Additionally, once you plant your little container or elevated bed, the weeds will come if you want it or not a cultivator functions as a fantastic tool to eliminate these youthful weeds as they germinate. When you are digging a planting hole, then a hand cultivator divides the ground more readily compared to a hand trowel. Much like a hand trowel, make certain to opt for a hand cultivator that feels comfortable on your hands which includes a grip firmly fastened to the blade. The steel-bladed kinds will be the most lasting.

Spades and Shovels

Spades and shovels are just two of the most widely used gardening gear. The gap between both is straightforward: A spade is created for grinding, and a spade was created for scooping and projecting. Shovels traditionally have curved and pointed blades, whereas spades possess flat, right, nearly rotating blades. A fantastic spade is vital in any garden for distributing dirt, manure, or compost. A spade is crucial for

151

trimming or breaking fresh ground. But many gardeners use spades for whatever from cutting dirt luggage to hammering in bets. Very good spades are rocky. The two spades and shovels arrive in brief - and - long-handled versions. An extended handle gives you more leverage when digging holes, so bear this in mind if you are buying a new spade.

Garden Forks

As useful as a spade is for turning new garden dirt, I find an iron fork is a much better instrument for turning beds which were worked before. The fork can slip into the ground as deep as 12 inches, and at precisely the exact same time divides clods and loosens and aerates the soil greater than a shovel. Iron forks look very similar to short-handled spades except they have three to four iron tines in their own heads. The top ones will be those forged from 1 piece of steel with wood grips firmly attached. They are great not just for turning dirt but also for turning compost piles and smelling root crops, like carrots and potatoes.

Garden Rakes

When you dig soil, you have to level it, split dirt clods, and eloquent that the seedbeds (particularly if you're climbing beds that are raised). An iron rake is an ideal tool for the job though you can use it for this purpose just a few times annually. A 14-inch-diameter, iron-toothed rake ought to have a long, wooden handle that is securely attached to a metallic head. You may turn the metallic head to actually smooth a seedbed level. To get a lightweight but less lasting version of an iron rake, then try out an aluminum rake.

Buckets, Wagons, also Baskets

You do not possess a 1,000-square-foot garden. However, you still should carry seeds, fertilizer, tools, create, and other things around. I enjoy speaking about storage containers since this is where the tools of this trade get very straightforward. Listed below are 3 fundamental containers:

✓ **Buckets:** For potting soil, fertilizers, and hand tools, a 5-gallon plastic bucket is the best container. You are likely to get one free in the building site simply be certain that you wash it out nicely. To get a more durable but smaller bucket, then purchase one made out of galvanized steel.

✓ **Wagons:** For lighter things, like apartments of seedlings, use a kid's old red wagon. Wagons are fantastic for transferring plants and tiny bags of compost in your garden, along with the lip to the wagon bed helps maintain these things in place when you pay bumpy ground. If you are considering a wagon to maneuver yourself (rather than just gear) around the garden, you can utilize a type of wagon which is a saddle using a chair. This sort of wagon generally has a swiveling chair and can be perched on four analog wheels, letting you sit down and push yourself throughout the garden as you operate. Its storage space under the chair too.

✓ **Baskets:** To collect that entire fantastic make you develop and harvest, put money into a cable or wicker basket. Wire baskets are easier to use as it is possible to wash the produce while it's still from the basket. Wicker and wooden baskets, even though more durable than steel, are more aesthetically pleasing and trendy in your garden. Piling your vegetables in a basket is much more functional than attempting to balance zucchinis on your arms while taking them out of the garden to your kitchen.

Chapter 2: What Is The Best Soil?

Soil

A rich calcium source, gypsum is essential for keeping your soil light and fluffy. It is especially useful for opening up heavy clay-based soils making them much easier to dig. Many gardeners ignore gypsum thinking that it is just used to break up clay soils, but gypsum also adds two important nutrients to your garden - calcium and Sulphur. Calcium is beneficial to the soil just as Sulphur. As a matter of fact, if you were to place all the nutrients in order of importance for plant health, Sulphur would be 9th and calcium 7th.

One of the key benefits of Sulphur is its ability to regulate the sodium in the soil. If your soil has too much sodium then the calcium becomes unavailable to your plants - no matter how much calcium you add to your soil!

Unlike agricultural and dolomite limes which do not dissolve into the soil and must be dug in to have any effect, the calcium in gypsum is water-soluble and immediately available to plant roots.

Gypsum loosens up compacted soils is because the Sulphur leeches excess sodium from the soil and replaces it with calcium. Plant roots are slower to grow in compacted soils, not because of the smaller pore space, but because compacted soils have too much sodium and excess sodium burns and discourage root development.

Gypsum also helps organic matter and nutrients move through soils, which is why gypsum-treated soils have deeper topsoil than soils where no gypsum has been applied. In short, if you want to create well-balanced deep black soils then you need to apply gypsum to your garden beds regularly.

Types of Soil

Clay Soil

This type of soil feels lumpy and may feel sticky too when wet and it is rock-hard when it is dry. Clay soils drain poorly and it has fewer air spaces. This type of soil is heavy to cultivate but if drainage is improved well, plants grow better because clay soil holds a lot of nutrients than any other soil.

Sandy Soil

This type of soil is free-draining soil and is gritty when you touch it. Unlike clay soil, sandy soil warms quickly in the spring season. It is easier to cultivate but this type of soil may lack out nutrients because nutrients are easily washed through the soil in wet weather.

Silty Soil

The Silty soil is smooth and soapy when you touch it. This is a well-drained soil and is richer in nutrients than sandy soil because Silty Soils have more fertile soil. The soil structure is weak but it is a very good soil if it is managed well.

Peaty Soil

This type of soil contains a much higher level of peat or proportion of organic matter because of the soil's acidic nature which inhibits decomposition. But even though this contains higher peat, this soil has fewer nutrients. It is dark in color and it warms up quickly in spring.

Chalky Soil

The chalky soil is alkaline with a pH level of 7.5 or more. This type of stone is usually stony and has free draining. This type of soil can be remedied by using fertilizers which will make minerals like Manganese and Iron available to the plants making the plants avoid the yellowing of the seeds.

Loamy Soil

The loamy soil is known as the perfect soil for gardening. This has a good structure and it drains well too. This also retains moisture and is also full of nutrients! This type of soil is easy to cultivate and it warms up quickly in spring but it does not dry out when it is summer. You can consider yourself a lucky gardener if you have this type of soil!

Fertilizing

Nitrogen, Potassium, and Phosphorus amounts vary greatly depending on the different seeds being used in the meal. Generally, seed meals with high protein content will have equally high concentrations of NPK, whereas low protein seeds will have lower NPK values. Here are the most common seed meals with their protein and NPK ratios:

• Neem - 34% protein with an NPK of 6-1-2 (my preferred seed meal)

• Alfalfa - 17% with 2-1-2

• Soy - 36% with 7-2-1

• Cotton - 33% with 5-2-1

You can find many different seed meals for cheap prices at livestock and farm supply stores, where they are sold as a livestock feed replacement. Seed meals are popular among farmers because the high carbohydrate content can quickly fatten an animal in the final weeks before they send it to slaughter.

Protecting Your Plants with Lime

Regularly adding lime to your garden soils is easily the single most important thing you can do to grow better vegetables. Adding lime to your soil will help your plants grow big and strong. Calcium, which is the main component in most limes, will ensure your plants grow strong cell walls, enabling them to fight off pests and diseases easily.

Even if your garden soil is alkaline, the addition of a small amount of lime in this fertilizer will not increase the pH of your soil, unless it is below 6.0. The pH scale is not a linear measurement from 1-14 like many people think, instead it is a logarithmic scale where each number is 10 times greater than the last.

Increasing your soil's pH with the addition of lime is easy in acidic soils that have a pH of less than 6.0, but the higher the pH the less effect lime has on the soil. High pH soils generally have a high level of calcium, but this calcium is locked up in unavailable forms which is why you still need to apply lime to even alkaline soils.

If you plan to use a chicken tractor or spreading compost over your beds then this will tend to make your soil more acidic over time. Vegetables like to grow in soils with a pH between 6 and 6.5, anything below 5 or above 7 tends to reduce the growth and yields of most vegetable crops.

Benefit Of Composting

The many benefits of compost include:

1. It Makes Plants Healthier

Expert gardeners call compost "black gold" for a reason. It is the single most effective thing that you can do to improve the quality of your soil. And high-quality, fertile soil makes all the difference when you are trying to grow something -- whether it is grass, trees, shrubs, flowers, fruits, or vegetables. Compost is alive -- it adds beneficial microbes and nutrients to your soil. Healthy soil results in more significant, more robust plants that fight off disease and flourish even in less-than-optimal conditions.

2. It's Good for the Environment

According to a study made by the Environmental Protection Agency, yard trimmings and food scraps make up 23 percent of the total garbage in the United

States. In 2000, 56.9 percent of those materials were composted. (Which is significant progress, because only 12 percent of those materials were composted ten years earlier, in 1990.) But that still means 43.1 percent of yard trimmings and food scraps go straight to the landfill, where they are entirely wasted. Landfill space is limited, and it costs money to put something there. Why throw stuff away at a great expense when we can turn it into rich compost instead? We must be responsible rather than dumping all our compostable materials into a landfill.

3. It Saves You Money

Making your own compost can reduce or eliminate the money you would otherwise spend to buy it from your local garden supply center. And compost that you make yourself is often better quality. Bagged compost is usually made from just one bulk material, like cow manure or cotton burrs. Compost that is made from a mix of yard and garden waste and food scraps has a wider variety of nutrients, which makes it richer and better for your soil.

Making your own compost saves money in other ways too. Plants growing in rich, healthy soil are naturally healthier, and not as susceptible to pests and plant diseases. This means you will spend less time and money on pest and disease control measures. And you will spend less money replacing plants that have died.

4. It Optimizes Soil Drainage

Do you have sandy soil that needs a lot of water to keep your plants happy? If so, then finished compost will act like a sponge, slowing down the drainage and keeping more water available for your plants. This means watering less often! Composted soil is also more resistant to erosion -- poor-quality soil washes away quickly when it is flooded, but rich soil is able to absorb water and release it later.

5. It Balances and Buffers Your Soil pH

You've probably read how most plants do best with a soil pH near neutral (7). Soil that is too acidic or too alkaline can prevent plant roots from absorbing essential nutrients. What happens when you add compost? The complex organic matter in compost helps to balance your soil and bring it closer to neutral, raising the pH of acidic soil and lowering the pH of alkaline soil. Compost also has the ability to absorb acid or alkaline additions to your soil, thus buffering your soil from sudden pH swings.

Types Of Composting

Backyard Or Onsite Composting

Homeowners, small businesses, and backyard garden enthusiasts can reduce their organic disposal costs by onsite composting. Yard trimmings and a wide variety of fresh food scraps can be composted right on the property. Commercial establishments and large institutions such as hospitals, universities, and prisons that generate huge quantities of food scraps may compost in situ if their campuses are big enough to allocate the space needed. When lawns are mowed regularly, the grass clippings can be left on the lawn to decompose naturally. This is known as grasscycling – the grass cuttings decay and enrich the turf. Onsite composters may rake up leaves into piles, and leave them to use later as mulch.

Very little time or equipment is required for backyard or onsite composting. Local residents may wish to educate one another by sharing composting tips and techniques.

Or they can organize composting demonstrations and seminars to educate and encourage their neighbors or businesses in their community to compost on their own properties. Converting organic material to compost may take as long as two years. Manual turning can accelerate the decomposition significantly to less than 6 months or less.

Compost Tea

Beneficial microbes are extracted from vermicomposting and other types of high-density microbial compost. Compost tea is made by steeping or soaking compost in water for three days to a week. Water, air, food, and comfort are the four essentials for microbes to flourish. The water used for compost tea must be clean and de-chlorinated. Pure drinking (potable) water is perfect. Air is mixed into the "brewing" by a system of pipes that delivers oxygen to the microbes. Packaged nutrient mixes are added to the liquid to feed the colonies of fungi and bacteria.

The "brewed" tea is sprayed on seedlings, on the non-edible parts of vegetation or it is worked into the soil as a drench to treat root tips. The microbes get down to work to suppress disease and help the soil retain moisture and nutrients. Compost tea controls some fungal plant diseases on plant leaves so it can replace some toxic garden pesticides and fungicides.

Leaf-Mold Tea Or Green Manure Tea

Some leguminous plants like beans, peanuts, soybeans, and other perennials are rich in nitrogen. A nutritious "tea" is made from the leaves of such plants. Many crop leaves and wild greens such as comfrey and tithonia (wild sunflower species) may also be used to make leaf-mold tea. To make leaf-mold tea, a small pile of shredded or mashed-up leaves is wrapped in cheesecloth, burlap, or any suitable material, including nylon netting. The packet is immersed in a large bucket of water. If the leaf packet threatens to float, it is weighed down with a rock or some bricks. It is left for three days or longer to steep or to brew. The "teabag" is unwrapped and the contents are dumped into the compost heap. Leaf-mold or green manure tea is splashed directly on plants. This tea is mild so it doesn't burn young plants, even seedlings.

<u>Vermicomposting</u>

Vermicomposting uses worms to break down organic matter in compost bins. Ordinary earthworms in the garden could be used (if you have the patience to dig them up and transfer them into the bin). A variety of worm species including earthworms, white worms, and red wigglers are used to produce vermicast. The worm poop, called castings, is high-value compost. This high-quality end-product is also known as worm manure, worm castings, and worm humus. (Paper on Invasive Worms)

Vermiculture experts prefer red wigglers because they are voracious eaters and they breed fast. Compared to conventional composting, vermicomposting produces compost quicker as worms convert organic matter to usable end-product faster. When earthworms digest their food, they mix up minerals and nutrients into simple forms that are easy for plants to absorb. Beneficial microbes in the worms' digestive tract help to efficiently break down food particles that eventually enrich the soil. Vermicast is less saline so it can be applied directly to plants without risking "burning" sensitive plant parts. (Lazcano, Gomez-Brandon and Dominguez 2008)

In-vessel Composting

This large-scale operation requires expensive concrete-lined trenches, silos, sturdy drums, and similar equipment to contain the organic matter to be composted. Aeration, moisture, and temperature are vigilantly monitored, often electronically. Unlike the weather constraints of windrow and static pile composting, in-vessel composting can be done in all and even extreme climatic conditions with proper insulation.

A mechanism in the composting vessel turns or agitates the organic matter to aerate it properly. Large volumes of any organic waste including biosolids, animal manure, food scraps, and meat or other animal byproducts can be accommodated in in-vessel composters. The vessels vary in size, some as large as a school bus and others small enough to fit into a restaurant or school kitchen.

Grub Composting

This is a very fast technique for making compost. Black soldier flies are kept in "cages" where they lay their eggs. The eggs hatch into larvae or grubs. Enthusiasts and breeders say grub composting can be done in the garage, the bedroom, and even the kitchen because the bins are sanitary and the whole operation is basically odorless and tidy. Grubs quickly convert kitchen waste and animal manure into usable compost. Grubs are at least 50 times more efficient than earthworms and other wigglers at composting waste.

It could be fascinating to watch masses of these creepy crawlies devour huge quantities of organic waste such as fruit peel and food scraps, meat, and even animal manure. Chopping and shredding would not be necessary. The voracious grubs are incredible eating machines - they consume almost everything, including rotting vegetation dumped into the bins. The sawdust-like and odorless grub poop is called fry, a useful compost residue. Earthworms love grub poop.

Cockroach Composting

Yes, cockroaches are amazingly efficient composters. Cockroaches can eat anything and everything, they reproduce like crazy, need only super-low maintenance, and don't smell. Cockroaches are difficult to kill except by using disastrous chemicals. You may find it disgusting to think of raising cockroaches to do composting, but, it's true, these hardy insects can convert kitchen waste and even manure into compost much faster than the traditional compost heap.

Species such as the Turkestan cockroach or Blaptica dubia, Blatta lateralis, and others are used. While cockroaches produce fewer droppings than other invertebrates used for composting, the castings are more nutrient-dense. At different stages, cockroaches molt, and the chitin from the molts boosts the quality of the compost. Excess insects can be fed to farm animals and pets like bearded dragons, geckos, and some birds.

Cockroach composting is unconventional, weird, and freaky. One has to overcome the initial disgust of cockroaches. But, the efficiency of these disgusting insects makes up for the prejudice targeted at them. A discarded aquarium tank or any large-enough container can be used as cockroach bins. All kinds of food can be tossed into the cockroach breeding pen - nasty moldy food, dog food, people food - all leftovers. Prolific breeders, a cockroach colony can grow at astonishing speed. Each capsule-looking egg case contains 20 to 30 eggs.

Aerated (turned) windrow composting

"Windrows" are long piles of organic waste laid out in the field. These long rows, 14 to 16 feet wide, are turned manually or mechanically from time to time to aerate them. Windrows need to be between 4 and 8 feet high for them to be sufficiently hot and still allow oxygen to reach the core. Aerated windrow composting accommodates huge quantities of organic wastes such as those generated by sizeable communities and businesses that process high volumes of food such as packing plants, restaurants, and cafeterias.

Diverse wastes such as yard trimmings, animal byproducts, grease, liquids, or slurry are incorporated in windrows that are turned frequently and carefully monitored by municipal environment agencies. Sturdy equipment and labor are needed. In cold climates, the outside portions of windrows may freeze but the core can maintain 140° F. To retain the moisture in windrows, shelters are sometimes built over the whole lengths of the windows.

During the rainy seasons, the piles are adjusted to allow water to drain off instead of seeping into the heap. Aerated windrow composting is a large-scale operation that requires proper environmental measures to address issues such as leachate that might contaminate ground and surface-water supplies, control of odors and pest infestation, community zoning, and other public health concerns. Windrow composting yields huge amounts of compost that some local governments give for free or very little cost to encourage more residents to do organic gardening.

Chapter 3: The "Lasagna" Method

Firstly, to clear up any confusion, Lasagna Gardening is known by a number of names including Layer Composting, Layer gardening, Sheet Composting, or Lasagna Composting. Call it what you like but it all adds up to the same thing.

Easy weed-free, no-till gardening, that uses up as much organic waste as you can provide, that will, in turn, produce an abundance of crops at very little expense in both materials and labor.

It can be used alongside or in conjunction with other small gardening ideas, such as Raised Bed Gardening or Container Gardening. And it can be used in any area of the garden that gets sufficient sunshine for plants to grow.

Although some would claim it is a new idea, it is in essence a modern twist on an ancient concept and has in fact been used under different names or descriptions since ancient times.

However, the title 'Lasagna Gardening' alongside the others mentioned are indeed the product of the late 19**th** century till now.

In essence, a Lasagna garden is a layered rubbish heap filled with organic material, either by accident or design. The ancient Scots for instance referred to this as a Midden. A place where all food waste and animal dung would be dumped.

It was most likely realized that some of the waste vegetables took root and thrived in these conditions, and soon the Midden itself was used to grow vegetable crops.

I myself have known of this method since I was a child, as my parents were both crofters in a remote area of Northern Scotland, near Montrose.

Of course, things have changed a lot since then, and the concept of growing healthy organic vegetables in a rubbish heap has 'evolved' into the Lasagna Gardening style (amongst others) as we now know it.

Advantages Of A Lasagna Veggie Garden

1: Excellent Re-cycling: This is a great way to convert any old organic waste into fresh vegetables! Old newspaper, cardboard boxes, kitchen waste, etc. These can all be gathered and used to build up your Lasagna vegetable garden.

2: No Digging Required: This is a classic form of no-till gardening. The materials are simply thrown onto a layered heap, and the seedling or seeds planted in the pile.

The material does not get turned over at all, and the only digging required is the actual act of digging a small hole to plant your seedlings.

3: No Weeding: At least for the first few months of use, the Lasagna garden does not require weeding. This is mainly due to the fact that you are using a 'clean' growing medium, instead of weed-seed infested topsoil.

Some weeds will eventually make their way onto your Lasagna garden heap, but these are easily pulled up from the soft composting material.

4: No Fertilizers required: As the layered heap decomposes it creates a nutrient-rich growing medium. This means that you save money and effort as the plants have all the nutrients they need to thrive.

It also means that you can grow 100% organic, chemical-free vegetables for the family!

5: An excellent use of non-productive land: If you are 'blessed' with hard Stoney or otherwise poor soil on which to grow anything, then this method could be just what you are looking for!

The layered garden can be laid out on any piece of ground – even concrete! Just mark out your area (more on this later) and pile on your materials to create a super-productive vegetable bed.

I could go on – but I'm sure you get the idea by now!

Building A Lasagna Garden

Now we get down to the 'nuts & bolts' of Lasagna gardening, and in particular how to go about the construction itself.

Step 1: Find a suitable position: As mentioned earlier, you do not need to worry about the suitability of the ground with regard to growing your vegetables. This means that *with regard to the actual growing* of the vegetables, there are really only two main criteria to satisfy, and they are water supply and natural daylight.

Of course, depending on your situation you may have to consider predation by rabbits, deer, or other critters that love to munch on fresh vegetables. You may even have to consider possible vandalism or theft.

With regards to the actual plants' needs though, sun, water, and nutrients are the main considerations. The nutrients are already taken care of as the heap decomposes, with perhaps the possibility of a 'top-up' with organic fertilizer or tea.

Make sure that you are near to a water supply, as it can be a real drag if you are having to manhandle gallons of water to keep your veggies from expiring!

Most vegetables need a minimum of 8 hours of sunlight to grow, so be sure to pick a suitable spot in the yard that is not too shaded to suit your particular choice of vegetables.

Also, you should avoid setting up your Lasagna garden under over-hanging branches or heavy dense foliage. This will not only take sunshine away from your plants but can also lead to disease or insect infestation (especially aphids) amongst your vegetables.

Step 2: Collect your materials: What should you include in your Lasagna garden? Basically, everything that you put into your compost heap can be put into a Lasagna garden.

This is a shortlist of materials that *should be* included in a compost pile or indeed lasagna garden.

Carbon (Dried Matter): Dried leaves, straw, wood chips, sawdust, dried grass, straw, cardboard, paper (not colored), small twigs.

Nitrogen (Green matter): Fruit & Vegetable scraps, lawn clippings, weeds, plant cuttings, animal manure (herbivores only), old flowers.

Materials *NOT to include* in your compost for a variety of reasons include...

Anything inorganic such as plastic, polythene, polystyrene, etc. This should be a no-brainer as neither of these things decomposes – but it has to be said :)

Pet Poop: Dog or cat droppings should NEVER be added to the compost heap, as this can add several disease organisms as well as larvae to the mix.

Fat, fish, meat, bones, and dairy products: Should definitely not be added as they will attract rats and mice. They will also putrefy rather than decompose, which will cause your compost to smell bad.

Coal ash: The ashes from coal contain large amounts of Sulfur which is bad news for most plants, however, timber ash contains potash which is good especially for fruiting plants.

Colored paper: The paper from glossy magazines or any other colored paper should not be included, as the colors contain many harmful or toxic chemicals.

Diseased plants: Never add diseased plants to the layers as they are likely to spread the disease to your new vegetables. Dispose of them by burning if possible.

Once you have gathered together a suitable quantity of material to form your Lasagna garden – it should preferably be enough to form a heap 18-24 inches deep – then it is time to layer it up.

Step 3: Assembling the materials: Once you have the materials assembled you should roughly sort them into two categories: browns and greens.

The way it all works is this. The 'brown' material allows for ventilation or aeration of the heap as well as adding carbon. The 'green' material adds all the needed nutrients such as nitrogen & potassium.

The more 'green' material you have, then the faster the heap will decompose, and indeed the hotter it will get in the process. This is the basic premise behind Hot Bed Gardening – an early-season gardening method.

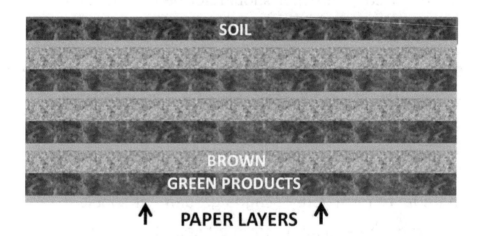

To make the Lasagna garden, I opt for a mix of approximately 3-4 parts 'brown' material to 1 part 'green.' This allows for a longer composting process and produces good results throughout the growing season.

The diagram below gives an example of a layered composting system. Whilst this looks nice and tidy in the diagram, the reality is that your Lasagna garden can look like a dog's breakfast – but not to worry :)

The layer of soil in the above diagram is optional, as shall be explained in the following part.

Grey Color = Paper or cardboard material (avoid glossy mags or rich colors).

Green = Organic nitrogen-rich vegetation such as grass cuttings, kitchen waste, manure, fruit, etc.

Light Brown = Carbon material such as wood shavings, sawdust, small twigs/branches, shredded newspaper.

Dark Brown = A 3-inch layer of compost or soil.

To set up the Lasagna system, start by laying out a few sheets of newspaper (5-10) or a layer of cardboard, and soak them thoroughly.

This can be laid directly over grass, weeds, whatever, as the paper/cardboard will stop the growth in its tracks.

I did mention earlier that you can even do this on top of concrete? This is true as you are not dependent on the surrounding soil in any way for your garden to operate. However, building it on concrete does lose the advantage of the natural process, where microbes and worms in *the* soil would help greatly in the composting process.

Yes, it will still function ok as nature gets to work, but for best results, it is better situated on soil or even a gravel bed.

On top of this layer of paper, pile a thick layer of brown material then your green material, then add to this your brown material. This is in turn topped by more paper or cardboard.

Repeat this process (watering throughout) until you have a layered bed at least 18 inches deep. Top-off the bed with a final layer of paper or cardboard.

Alternatively, if you want to begin growing vegetables immediately, top off the heap with 2-3 inches of good topsoil or better still a good growing medium such as a compost/peat/sand mix at 1/3**rd** each.

What now?

At this point there are a couple of choices open to you, depending on your particular circumstances.

If it happens to be the beginning of the growing season for you, then you can actually begin planting immediately by either topping off the pile with top-soil as previously described. Or alternatively, just dig a small pot-sized hole in the top layer and fill it with soil to get your plants started.

If it is later in the season and you need to leave it for a few months before starting, then you can either just walk away and let the whole mix rot-down; or you can cover it over with a tarp and leave it till spring. This will speed up the decomposition process and allow the worms and microbes to do their thing undisturbed.

Remove the tarp in the spring and plant your veggies!

Bear in mind that as the heap decomposes, the level will drop significantly over the ensuing weeks/months. This is to be expected and is merely a sign that the composting process is going as hoped.

Bit of a mess? Well yes, it can look a bit of an untidy mess, however, there are at least 3 simple solutions if you like your veggie plot to be nice and neat – and you don't mind a little extra work.

The first method is to simply create a wooden frame or box exactly the same as you would for a Raised Bed garden, and fill it in with the Lasagna composting method as described.

In the picture above you can see an example of a Raised Bed that is 2 feet high – which makes it easy on the 'old back,' since there is not a lot of bending over needed!

This box can be made using numerous different materials, anything that will contain the 'mess' within will do fine. Even chicken mesh can be used effectively to contain the infill. In fact, this method helps in the composting process as it allows air into the heap.

The Raised Bed example above is admittedly large; however, you can build it to any size that suits your needs – or material supply!

Another method which is perhaps more physical work but is less expensive to do is the 'trench style' Lasagna garden.

This involves digging out a hole or trench to the dimensions needed. Infill the organic material in exactly the same way as described earlier until it is 4 inches or so from the surface ground level.

Finish off by adding topsoil or growing mix until it is 2-3 inches proud of the surrounding ground level. This will compensate to some extent the sinking effect as decomposition takes place. At the end of the season, the pit can be topped up again to level it up with the rest of the veggie plot.

Yet another way, is in fact a combination of the first 2 methods. Instead of digging a pit 18-24 inches deep – which can involve some serious hard work, split the difference by digging a shallow pit only 6-12 inches deep and surround with a wooden frame to make up the difference.

For instance, a pit dug at 6 inches deep will need a 12-18 inches frame on top of the pit to make up a minimum of 18 inches of composting material.

The diagram above provides an example of a semi-sunken pit for Lasagna gardening. As an addition to this especially if you have water-logged or boggy ground, you could consider digging a sump at the bottom of the pit and filling it with loose stones or crushed gravel to act as a drain.

The bottom line is that there is little you can do 'wrong' when building your Lasagna garden. Just get a good mix of brown and green materials together and pile them up in an approximation of the manner described, and you will have a nutrient-rich bed in which to grow your veggies.

This method is also applicable to containers of many shapes and sizes, providing the container is large enough to infill with multiple layers of organic materials.

Planting Guide

So, what exactly can you grow in a layered garden? The answer to this is easy – virtually anything that can be grown in a traditional garden!

Ok, so this is somewhat dependent on how you go about planting your veggies, to begin with.

For instance, if you are planting straight into the top of the heap with no covering of soil, then I would not try growing deep-rooted plants such as carrots or parsnips

– at least not until the heap has had several months to break down.

The reason for this is that the roots will immediately hit obstructions from the cardboard or other brown material. This will result in the root going off in different directions, in much the same way as it would if you planted it in Stoney soil. See the pic below...

I'm fairly sure you will agree that this is not a good look :) It is however easily avoided by either waiting for a few months (build it late autumn and plant it out in the spring) for the material to break down thereby allowing the roots 'safe passage' or by using the following method.

With a garden knife or sharp spade, cut down into the top of the heap at least 6 inches then move the spade from side to side so that a 'V' shaped channel is formed in the heap.

Fill this in with a good compost mix before sprinkling a thin row of seeds along with it. This will create a perfect environment for your carrots to grow in and should result in healthy, straight roots.

This is exactly the same method as you would use when growing carrots or parsnips in a Straw Bale vegetable garden, and it is extremely effective.

There are of course many hundreds of different vegetables you can grow yourself, depending on factors such as your location, growing outside or in a hothouse, or indeed what you personally like or prefer to grow.

Written as a general guide to planting vegetables in a 'normal' garden set-up, it should be noted that vegetables grown in a Lasagna garden can be planted closer together than usual. This is due to several factors as listed below.

1. The growing medium is nutrient-rich; therefore, the plants are not fighting other plants for nutrients.
2. The fact that weeds are not so much of a problem in this gardening technique, means that you do not need to allow space for a garden hoe to get through.
3. As in point 1- The fact is that the veggies are not competing with weeds for nutrients and water.

Chapter 4: Easy To Grow Plants For Beginners

Warm Season and Cool Season Vegetables

You'll find information on plant families, feeding characteristics, and what pest and pathogen problems may affect each species. The plants are listed alphabetically, and this information should help you decide what vegetables you want to grow in your garden.

You can grow your own rainbow of crops!

Beans

- warm-season crop of the legume family
- light feeder, returns nitrogen to the soil
- pests: beetles, slugs, whiteflies, and cutworms
- pathogens: powdery mildew, white mold, mosaic virus
- sowing: direct sow after the threat of frost has passed
- planting: place seeds 1" deep, 2"-3" apart, rows separated by 18"
- harvest: pick when beans are as thick as a pencil
- storage: eat fresh within a week; freeze or can long-term
- quick info: the more you harvest, the more they'll produce

Beets

- cool-season crop of the beetroot family
- light feeder
- pests: leaf miners, leafhoppers, flea beetles
- pathogens: leaf spot, mosaic virus
- sowing: direct sow in early spring, once it hits 50 degrees

- planting: place seeds ½" deep, 2"-3" apart, rows separated by 12"
- harvest: best at 55-70 days, when roots are golf to tennis ball-size
- storage: eat fresh within a week; prepare and can, or dry store
- quick info: thin beet seedlings by snipping young greens for salads

Broccoli

- cool-season crop of the brassica family
- heavy feeder
- pests: aphids, cabbage worms, whiteflies
- pathogens: clubroot, white rust
- sowing: indoors in early spring, direct sow 3 weeks after last frost
- planting: place seeds ½" deep, 3" apart, rows no closer than 12"
- harvest: after 85 days, best picked in the morning
- storage: eat fresh within 5 days; prepare and freeze long-term
- quick info: keep the heads dry when watering to avoid rot

Brussels Sprouts

- cool-season crop of the brassica family
- heavy feeder
- pests: aphids, cabbage worms, whiteflies
- pathogens: clubroot, downy mildew, white mold
- sowing: indoors in early spring, direct sow 3 weeks after last frost
- planting: place seeds ½" deep, 2"-3" apart, rows no closer than 12"
- harvest: when globes are 1"-2" around
- storage: eat fresh within a week; freeze or can long-term
- quick info: encourage larger globes by trimming back top leaves

Cabbage

- cool-season crop of the brassica family
- heavy feeder
- pests: aphids, cabbage worms, loopers, cutworms, whiteflies
- pathogens: clubroot, downy mildew
- sowing: indoors in early spring, transplant when cloudy

- planting: carefully place seedlings no closer than 12"
- harvest: around 70 days, mature heads will begin to split
- storage: eat fresh within two weeks; dry storage for three months
- quick info: very heavy feeders- don't place them too close together

Carrots

- warm-season crop of the parsley family
- light feeder
- pests: carrot rust flies, flea beetles, wireworms
- pathogens: black canker, yellow aster disease (both rare)
- sowing: direct sow 3-5 weeks before last frost
- planting: place seeds ¼" deep, 2"-3" apart, in rows 12" apart
- harvest: when carrots are at least a half-inch thick
- storage: seal fresh carrots in airtight bags; freeze, can, or dry-store
- quick info: smaller=sweeter; carrots can withstand frost

Cauliflower

- cool-season crop of the brassica family
- heavy feeder
- pests: aphids, cabbage worms, whiteflies
- pathogens: clubroot, powdery mildew, white rust
- sowing: best results from nursery stock, plant before last frost
- planting: transplant 18-24" inches apart, in wide rows
- harvest: 80 days from transplant, when heads firm and tighten
- storage: eat fresh within a week; prepare and freeze long-term
- quick info: tie leaves up overhead a week before harvest to protect

Cucumbers

- warm-season crop of the cucurbit family
- medium feeder
- pests: aphids, cucumber beetles, squash bugs
- pathogens: blossom end rot, powdery mildew
- sowing: indoors, three weeks before transplant

- planting: when the soil reaches 70 degrees, 3" apart in narrow rows
- harvest: when fruits reach 2" (picklers) to 8" long (salad)
- storage: eat fresh within a week; pickle and can long-term
- quick info: harvest early and often to maximize each plant's output

Eggplant

- warm-season crop of the nightshade family
- medium feeder

- pests: flea beetles, hornworms
- pathogens: powdery mildew
- sowing: indoors in early spring, transplant 2 weeks after last frost
- planting: 2'-3' apart, in rows 3'-4' apart- need lots of space
- harvest: 65- 80 days after transplant, when fruits are firm/shiny
- storage: in the refrigerator for one week, take care not to break the skin
- quick info: stake or cage the plants when the fruit gets heavy

Kale

- cool-season crop of the brassica family
- light feeder
- pests: aphids, cabbage worms, flea beetles,
- pathogens: few known
- sowing: direct sow, 2-4 weeks before last frost
- planting: sow seeds ½" deep, thin young seedlings to 12" apart

- harvest: one 'fistful' at a time, do not harvest center bud
- storage: wash and refrigerate in a loose bag for one week
- quick info: eat raw or wilted, kale is rich in vitamins and minerals

Lettuce

- cool-season crop of the aster (daisy) family
- medium feeder

- pests: aphids, cutworms, earwigs, plus rabbits and woodchucks
- pathogens: white mold
- sowing: direct sow, after the weather is consistently over 40 degrees
- planting: sow seeds ½" deep, thin young seedlings to 12" apart
- harvest: Loose-leaf – cut outer leaves as wanted, or the whole head
  Crisp-head – when the head is firm, and leaves begin to peel
- storage: wash and refrigerate in a loose bag for one week
- quick info: lettuce will bolt and reseed itself if unharvested

Peas

- cool to early warm-season crop of the legume family
- light feeder, returns nitrogen to the soil
- pests: aphids, bean beetles, wireworms

- pathogens: downy mildew, fusarium wilt, powdery mildew
- sowing: direct sow, 4 weeks before last frost
- planting: place seeds 1" deep, 2" apart, in 2' wide rows
- harvest: 60-70 days, always harvest full stem to protect pods
- storage: eat fresh within a week; freeze, can, or dry pods long-term
- quick info: pea flowers are delicate, fragrant, and draw pollinators

Peppers

- warm-season crop of the nightshade family
- medium feeder
- pests: aphids, flea beetles, hornworms, potato beetles
- pathogens: anthracnose, blossom end rot, mosaic virus
- sowing: indoors in early spring, transplant 4 weeks after last frost

- planting: harden off before planting, space 18"-24" apart
- harvest: 80-100 days, the color will change the longer it remains on the plant
- storage: eat fresh within a week; freeze or dehydrate long-term
- quick info: the heat in a pepper comes from capsaicin in the seeds

Potatoes

- full season crop of the nightshade family
- medium feeder
- pests: aphids, flea beetles, potato beetles,
- pathogens: early or late blight, potato scab (pH imbalance)
- sowing: plant seed potatoes 4-6 weeks before last frost
- planting: place 3' apart, mound soil over roots as the plant grows
- harvest: 2-6 weeks after flowering, based on the desired size
- storage: eat fresh within 2 weeks; dry store long-term

- quick info: don't eat 'green' potatoes, they are mildly toxic

Pumpkins

- full season crop of the cucurbit family
- medium feeder
- pests: aphids, cucumber beetles, squash vine borers
- pathogens: anthracnose, powdery mildew
- sowing: direct sow, one month after last frost
- planting: place 4 seeds in a hill, with hills 12" apart, thin seedlings
- harvest: when full-size, deep in color, and hollow-sounding
- storage: use fresh for cooking; dry store long-term
- quick info: don't forget to roast the seeds; delicious and nutritious!

Radishes

- multi-harvest crop of the brassica family
- medium feeder
- pests: cabbage root maggots
- pathogens: clubroot
- sowing: direct sow in spring or fall
- planting: places seeds in a shallow trench, thin young seedlings
- harvest: 21-28 days, when roots are 1" round
- storage: eat fresh raw or cooked; freeze or dry store long-term
- quick info: radishes greens are also edible, raw, or pan-wilted

Spinach

- cool-season crop of the amaranth family
- heavy feeder
- pests: leaf miners
- pathogens: blight, downy mildew, mosaic virus
- sowing: direct sow immediately after last frost
- planting: place seeds in short rows, 12 seeds per 1", thin later

- harvest: when desired leaf size, either as needed or a whole head
- storage: wash and refrigerate in a loose bag for one week
- quick info: the larger the leaves, the more bitter the taste

Swiss Chard

- cool or warm-season crop of the beetroot family
- light feeder
- pests: aphids, leaf miners, slugs
- pathogens: leaf spot
- sowing: direct sow, 2-3 weeks before last frost
- planting: place seeds ½" deep, 2"-6" apart in narrow rows
- harvest: cut-as-you-go for chard all season, take outer leaves first
- storage: wash and refrigerate in a loose bag for one week
- quick info: plants over 1' tall will begin to lose flavor, harvest early

Sweet Potatoes

- full season crop of the bindweed (morning glory) family
- light to medium feeder
- pests: flea beetles
- pathogens: blight, leaf spot, scurf
- sowing: direct sow seed slips after the threat of frost has passed
- planting: place slips in 6" mounds, at least 12" apart
- harvest: after 100 days, or when the leaves and vines go yellow
- storage: eat fresh within days; cure well for long-term dry storage
- quick info: rich in Vitamin A; don't wash for better curing of skin

Tomatoes

- warm-season crop of the nightshade family
- heavy feeder
- pests: aphids, flea beetles, hornworms, whiteflies
- pathogens: blight, blossom end rot, mosaic virus

- sowing: indoors, in early spring
- planting: space seedlings no closer than 18", after last frost
- harvest: when fruit plumps and reddens, be gentle!
- storage: eat fresh within a week; process and can long-term
- quick info: stake or cage plants early to avoid damage

Winter Squash

- full season crop of the cucurbit family
- medium feeder
- pests: aphids, cucumber beetles, squash bugs, squash vine borer
- pathogens: blossom end rot, powdery mildew
- sowing: outdoors, 2-4 weeks after last frost, later for fall harvest
- planting: place 3-4 seeds in hills 6" apart, thin seedlings
- harvest: when fruits are medium-sized and firm

- storage: winter squash can be cured and stored for up to 3 months
- quick info: varieties include butternut, acorn, and spaghetti

Zucchini/Summer Squash

- warm-season crop of the cucurbit family
- medium feeder
- pests: aphids, cucumber beetles, squash bugs, squash vine borer
- pathogens: blossom end rot, powdery mildew
- sowing: outdoors, 2 weeks after last frost
- planting: place 3-4 seeds in hills 6" apart, thin seedlings
- harvest: when fruits are 10-12" long, larger will be pithy and bitter
- storage: eat fresh within a week; prepare and freeze long-term
- quick info: zucchini is prolific, bake lots of zucchini bread!

As you can see from this list, there are commonalities in the characteristics of plants in the same families. Being able to recognize their connections can help you be a better garden designer, diagnostician, and troubleshooter. Learning to grow the basic varieties of these vegetables will also give you the experience you need to branch out and try new cultivars and varieties, opening up a whole new world of fresh food for you to enjoy!

Herbs

Garlic

- Extra Easy, Container-Friendly, Raised Bed–Friendly
- Family: Amaryllidaceae
- Growing zones: N/A
- Growing season(s): cool weather
- Spacing: 6 to 8 inches
- Start indoors or direct sow: direct sow
- Indoor sowing date: N/A
- Earliest outdoor planting: 2 weeks before the average first frost
- Soil temperature: N/A
- Fall planting: N/A

- Sun needs: 6+ hours
- Water needs: low
- Harvest category: one harvest

Suggested varieties for beginners: soft-neck for warmer regions, hard-neck for cooler regions

Keep in Mind Tip: Although it's possible to plant garlic cloves you buy at the grocery store; I don't recommend it. First, this garlic is usually not certified disease-free, so you risk contaminating your garden soil for years to come. Second, you don't know whether that variety will grow in your region. Most garlic in grocery stores are soft-neck garlic, which grows well in the South but doesn't tolerate cold as well as hard-neck types.

Snapshot

Garlic is one of the easiest crops for a home gardener to grow. Planted in the fall for the following season, garlic requires little maintenance and is one of the first plants to begin growing in the early spring. An adaptable crop, garlic can be grown in the ground, in raised beds, and in containers.

Starting

Purchase certified disease-free bulbs of garlic from a reputable seed supplier. At around the time of your first fall frost, separate individual cloves from the bulb and plant pointy-side up in 2-inch-deep trenches. Cover with soil, and in cold-climate areas, spread an additional 1 to 2 inches of mulch. Water well at planting.

Growing

Garlic will likely sprout in the fall, stop growing through the winter, and start growing again in the late winter. Water isn't necessary during this dormant period; begin consistent light irrigation in the spring if rainfall is scarce. Keep the area well weeded (mulch helps).

Harvesting and Storing

Southern gardeners may start harvesting garlic in mid-May; northern growers may not harvest until late July. In either case, watch for the lower half of the leaves to turn brown and die off. Use a trowel to dig around the bulb to loosen the soil. Pull out the bulbs and move them to a shaded, well-ventilated location (such as a garage). Lay the bulbs in single layers or hang them. Set a fan on them if you live in a humid location and let them "cure" for 2 to 4 weeks. Curing is complete when the necks of the bulbs completely dry out. Clip the bulbs from the dry foliage, trim the roots, and move them to a root cellar or pantry for storage. Save the biggest bulbs in a loosely closed brown paper bag for your next crop.

Common Problem

Garlic usually has few problems. Abnormally rainy springs can cause poor bulb development, as can planting the cloves too close together. If you live in a wet area, plant garlic in raised beds or containers.

Onions

- Container-Friendly, Raised Bed–Friendly
- Family: Amaryllidaceae
- Growing zones: N/A
- Growing season(s): cool weather
- Spacing: 6 inches
- Start indoors or direct sow: start indoors or purchase transplants or sets
- Indoor sowing date: 10 weeks before transplant (16 weeks before average last frost)

- Earliest outdoor planting: 6 weeks before average last frost
- Soil temperature: 50° to 95°
- Fall planting: N/A
- Sun needs: 6+ hours
- Water needs: moderate
- Harvest category: one harvest
- Suggested varieties for beginners: Ailsa Craig (long-day), Yellow Granex (short-day)

Keep in Mind Tip: If you want to eat "green onions" (scallions), you can harvest the leaves at any time. Just keep in mind that those leaves help nourish the developing bulb; the more leaves you remove, the smaller the bulb will be. Consider planting a crop just for scallions that you can harvest throughout the season.

Snapshot

Onions are one of the most commonly used vegetables for cooking. The key to growing good onions is to choose the correct seeds, sets, or transplants for your area. In order to harvest a large bulb, gardeners in the southern United States must grow short-day onions, and gardeners in the North must grow long-day ones.

Gardeners in the middle parts of the country can try either type or purchase "day-neutral" varieties.

Starting

Most beginning gardeners plant onions from transplants or sets. Transplants look like scallions from the grocery store; sets look like baby onion bulbs. Most sets are long-day onions, so if you live in the South, double-check the variety or your onions won't bulb. Plant onions in well-drained soil amended with plenty of organic matter. Transplants should be planted with the white part underground; bury sets just beneath the soil's surface.

Growing

Keep the area well weeded. In the early months of growth, rainfall will likely provide sufficient water, but during hotter times of year or periods of drought, ensure onions receive 1 to 2 inches of irrigation per week. After the soil has warmed, apply a layer of mulch to help with weed control and to conserve moisture.

Harvesting and Storing

Onions are ready to harvest when the tops have yellowed and fallen over. Dig out the bulbs, being careful not to stab them with the trowel. Transfer them to a shaded, well-ventilated location where you can lay them in single layers or hang them. Let them "cure" until the stems have dried out and no moisture remains in the stem when you clip off the foliage. Store in a cool area such as a root cellar or the bottom of your pantry.

Common Problem

If the onion plant sends out a tall flower stalk before it's ready to harvest, the plant has bolted and bulb production has stopped. Early bolting is typically caused by environmental stress such as extreme temperature fluctuations or water issues. Keep the area mulched to moderate soil temperature. Upon bolting, harvest the onion bulbs and use them before other onions, because they will not store well.

Basil

- Extra Easy, Quick, Container-Friendly, Raised Bed–Friendly
- Family: Lamiaceae
- Growing zones: N/A
- Growing season(s): warm weather
- Spacing: 12 inches
- Start indoors or direct sow: either, or purchase transplants
- Indoor sowing date: 4 weeks before average last frost
- Earliest outdoor planting: after last spring frost
- Soil temperature: 60° to 90°
- Fall planting: N/A

- Sun needs: 6+ hours
- Water needs: moderate
- Harvest category: all season
- Suggested varieties for beginners: sweet basil, cinnamon basil, Genovese

Preparation Tip: Turn extra basil into a simple pesto. Combine 20 to 30 basil leaves, ¼ cup of olive oil, 2 garlic cloves, ½ teaspoon of salt, ¼ teaspoon of pepper, 1 tablespoon of pine nuts, and 2 tablespoons of Parmesan cheese in a food processor or blender and blend to a paste. Serve over angel-hair pasta or make larger batches to freeze.

Snapshot

Possibly the most popular herb in the home garden, basil is beloved for its fragrant and tasty leaves. Enjoyed fresh in Italian dishes or made into basil pesto, no home garden should be without this summer delight.

Starting

Basil thrives in warm weather. It will die in a frost and suffer damage when nights dip below 50°. For this reason, wait to plant basil (seeds or transplants) until a week or more after your last frost. If direct sowing, scatter seeds on top of the soil and scrape them in with your fingers. Water well and keep moist until germination.

Growing

Keep basil consistently moist but not waterlogged. For an all-season harvest, keep the plant trimmed, starting at about 6 inches high so it will bush out. Trim the tips of the stems when the leaves start forming a tight cluster in the center. Without proper pruning, those clusters will bloom into flowers (and eventually seeds), and the quality of the remaining leaves will decline.

Harvesting and Storing

Harvest basil early and often, and use fresh leaves immediately. If you need to store the leaves, cut them with stems that are long enough to place them upright in a glass of water in the refrigerator.

Common Problem

Basil loves to flower and go to seed quickly. But pollinators and beneficial insects love those flowers. Get the best of both worlds by planting multiple plants, keeping one trimmed for fresh use, and letting the others flower. When the flower pods dry out, gather the seeds to save for next season.

Cilantro

- Quick, Container-Friendly, Raised Bed–Friendly
- Family: Apiaceae
- Growing zones: N/A
- Growing season(s): cool weather
- Spacing: 6 inches
- Start indoors or direct sow: direct sow
- Indoor sowing date: N/A
- Earliest outdoor planting: as soon as soil can be worked
- Soil temperature: 55° to 68°
- Fall planting: 4 to 6 weeks before the average first frost
- Sun needs: 6+ hours
- Water needs: moderate
- Harvest category: weather dependent
- Suggested varieties for beginners: Slo-bolt, Santo

Fun Fact: Does cilantro taste like soap to you? It's not just you. A certain percentage of the population has a genetic sensitivity to aldehydes in cilantro leaves, which makes them perceive the flavor as soapy.

Snapshot

A love-it-or-hate-it herb, cilantro is a staple in many gardens. Cilantro, unlike the foods it's usually paired with, hates hot weather, and prefers the cool temperatures of fall, winter, and spring.

Starting

Sow cilantro seeds directly into the garden about 2 inches apart, thinning to 6 inches apart. Cilantro likes well-drained soil enriched with compost. Plant several plants if you plan to freeze or preserve them.

Growing

If you live in a hotter climate, mulch the plants well and consider afternoon shade to keep soil temperatures as low as possible for as long as possible.

Harvesting and Storing

Start harvesting cilantro when it's 6 inches tall. When the plant starts to bolt and flower, leave it, and you can harvest the seeds as the spice coriander.

Common Problem

Cilantro bolts quickly in warm weather, so harvest it frequently while it's small. The leaves turn bitter when they become feathery and the center stalk starts growing tall. Sow succession plantings to keep a continuous supply, then let the bolted plants flower and go to seed. As the plants drop the seed they may continuously self-sow. If you grow cilantro in the fall, you may have a longer harvest window.

Mint

- Extra Easy, Quick, Container-Friendly
- Family: Lamiaceae
- Growing zones: N/A
- Growing season(s): perennial in zones 3 (some varieties) +
- Spacing: 12 to 18 inches
- Start indoors or direct sow: purchase transplants
- Indoor sowing date: N/A
- Earliest outdoor planting: early spring
- Soil temperature: N/A
- Fall planting: N/A

- Sun needs: 6+ hours
- Water needs: high
- Harvest category: all season
- Suggested varieties for beginners: peppermint, spearmint, chocolate mint, lemon balm

Fun Fact: Peppermint is a well-known tummy soother. Pinch off fresh leaves and steep them in hot water for 10 minutes. Add honey if desired. (Not recommended for young children.)

Snapshot

Mints of all kinds are a delight in the garden. Just make sure to plant them in a well-contained place, as the plants spread invasively. Containers are the best solution. Use mint in hot tea, summertime fruit salads, and in cold, refreshing mint water. Once you learn the variety of uses for homegrown mint, you'll be glad you added it to your garden.

Starting

Purchase potted mint from your local garden center and plant it in rich, moist soil. It requires more water than other herbs, so consider this when combining herbs in large pots or beds.

Growing

Besides keeping mint plants well-watered (especially during the heat of the summer), the best care you can provide is pruning. Cut the plants frequently to keep them producing tender new leaves.

Harvesting and Storing

Cut mint as needed for fresh use. If it becomes woody, cut back the entire plant to promote new growth (you can do this a few times throughout the season). Dry the cuttings in a dehydrator or hang them upside down in a dark, airy location. Strip the leaves and store them in clean jars.

Common Problem

If your mint plant stops growing and seems to show woody rather than tender growth, most likely it has outgrown its pot. Wait for mild weather (not high heat or winter cold) and take the entire plant out of the pot. Divide it with a sharp knife and replant one division in fresh soil. Plant the other division in a separate container (or give to a friend). Water it well.

Parsley

- Quick, Container-Friendly, Raised Bed–Friendly
- Family: Apiaceae
- Growing zones: N/A
- Growing season(s): cool-weather biennial
- Spacing: 10 inches
- Start indoors or direct sow: either, or purchase transplants
- Indoor sowing date: 4 weeks before transplant (6 weeks before average last frost)
- Earliest outdoor planting: 2 weeks before average last frost
- Soil temperature: 50° to 80°
- Fall planting: in the South, plant transplants 4 weeks before first frost
- Sun needs: 4+ hours
- Water needs: moderate
- Harvest category: all season, weather dependent in some areas
- Suggested varieties for beginners: Italian dark green, curly parsley

Fun Fact: Whether parsley bolts in the first year or completes its growing cycle in the second year, if left to flower and drop seed, it may self-sow, giving you a continuous supply.

Snapshot

Parsley is said to intensify other flavors. However, the flavor profile amplifies when you grow it yourself. Dried parsley and store-bought parsley simply do not compare to the homegrown herb. When parsley is established and grown under ideal conditions, you can expect to harvest it for well over a year, until its growth cycle causes it to flower and set seed in its second year.

Starting

Though you can sow parsley from seed, it can take a long time to germinate. Many first-time gardeners prefer to purchase transplants. Plant parsley in moist but well-drained soil with plenty of organic matter.

Growing

Keep plants evenly watered. In the hotter summers of the South, parsley benefits from afternoon shade, because high temperatures and water stress can cause it to bolt in the first year. Southern growers may find fall planting to be more successful and will be able to harvest leaves all winter.

Harvesting and Storing

Begin harvesting when the plant reaches 6 inches in height, and harvest as needed. Or, for a larger harvest for drying, cut the plant back to 1 to 2 inches above soil level, where it will regrow leaves. Parsley can be dried, but the flavor will weaken considerably.

Common Problem

When the plant produces a tall center stalk, it has bolted. The leaves can still be used, though the flavor might become bitter. To prevent parsley from bolting, mulch the plants well and keep them watered to limit stress, especially in the hot summer.

Rosemary

- Extra Easy, Quick, Container-Friendly, Raised Bed–Friendly
- Family: Lamiaceae
- Growing zones: N/A
- Growing season(s): perennial in zones 7+

- Spacing: 36 inches
- Start indoors or direct sow: purchase transplants
- Indoor sowing date: N/A
- Earliest outdoor planting: early spring
- Soil temperature: N/A
- Fall planting: N/A
- Sun needs: 4+ hours
- Water needs: low
- Harvest category: all season (zones 7+), weather dependent (zones 6-)
- Suggested varieties for beginners: N/A

Troubleshooting Tip: Rosemary may not survive outdoors where temperatures dip below 5°; gardeners in borderline zones may have success planting rosemary in a southern-exposure location or in the ground with heavy mulch. Northern gardeners can bring rosemary pots inside for the winter.

Snapshot

A beautifully fragrant shrub, rosemary is perfect for a container patio garden and mixes well with other herbs. Light, well-drained soil is best for the plant, and it tolerates drought. After a few years, rosemary will become tough and woody; plan to replace old plants every few years for the best-quality herb.

Starting

Purchase a potted transplant from a local garden center. Water it well at transplant and it shouldn't have any trouble getting established.

Growing

Rosemary grown in the ground rarely requires supplemental irrigation. Potted rosemary should be monitored occasionally to ensure the soil doesn't dry out completely.

Harvesting and Storing

Snip leaves as necessary for fresh use. To harvest for storage purposes, cut the stems a few inches above where they have become woody, but don't harvest more than one-third of the plant at a time. Hang the cuttings upside down in a dark, airy location. When they're dry, strip the leaves and store them in a clean jar.

Common Problem

If the leaves turn brown, the plant likely received too much water. To avoid this problem, cut down on watering or, if the plant is outside, move it to a sheltered location during rainy periods or mulch it to help moderate the moisture.

<u>Sage</u>

- Extra Easy, Quick, Container-Friendly, Raised Bed–Friendly
- Family: Lamiaceae
- Growing zones: N/A
- Growing season(s): perennial in zones 4 to 8
- Spacing: 18 inches
- Start indoors or direct sow: purchase transplants
- Indoor sowing date: N/A
- Earliest outdoor planting: early spring
- Soil temperature: N/A
- Fall planting: N/A
- Sun needs: 6+ hours
- Water needs: low
- Harvest category: all season
- Suggested varieties for beginners: culinary sage

Fun Fact: Sage can be grown indoors on a sunny windowsill, giving you a fresh supply of the herb all winter. Choose a compact variety and cut back any flowers that form.

Snapshot

Sage is most commonly known as the spice in Thanksgiving dressing, but it's also a staple in sausage, meatloaf, and pork dishes. In most zones, sage grows as a perennial. It may lose its leaves in the winter but will regrow in the spring. In areas that don't receive frost, sage may not grow year-round because of a lack of chilling time needed for new growth.

Starting

Purchase a potted sage plant at your local garden center and plant it in light, well-drained soil. Water it well at planting.

Growing

Sage prefers full sun, but it may need partial shade in areas with hot summers. After the first year, cut back the entire plant to half its size after new growth begins to appear. This will keep the plant in check and also encourage new tender growth.

Harvesting and Storing

Pick sage leaves as needed for fresh use. Sage leaves can also be dried when cut back in the second year and ground into a spice.

Common Problem

Once established, sage prefers not to have a lot of water. If the soil is too heavy and rainfall causes it to stay saturated, it can show signs of disease. If you have a heavier soil, add sand or perlite to help with drainage.

<u>Thyme</u>

- Extra Easy, Quick, Container-Friendly, Raised Bed–Friendly
- Family: Lamiaceae
- Growing zones: N/A

- Growing season(s): perennial in zones 4+
- Spacing: 12 inches
- Start indoors or direct sow: purchase transplants
- Indoor sowing date: N/A
- Earliest outdoor planting: early spring
- Soil temperature: N/A
- Fall planting: N/A
- Sun needs: 4+ hours
- Water needs: low
- Harvest category: all season
- Suggested varieties for beginners: common thyme, English thyme, creeping thyme

Keep in Mind Tip: Because thyme will make its home in most gardens for several years, choose its location carefully.

Snapshot

A fuss-free, low-growing herb, thyme can grow in a trailing fashion or like a shrub. In zones 4 and above, thyme is a hardy perennial, and you can harvest from an established plant year-round.

Starting

Purchase potted thyme from your local nursery. Plant in well-draining soil; a container is a perfect choice.

Growing

Besides the initial watering, thyme requires little extra care. If you live in zone 4, mulch the plants before winter to protect them from the cold. Thyme doesn't like too much moisture, so mulch with fine gravel or pine needles instead of wood mulch.

Harvesting and Storing

Thyme can be harvested for fresh eating year-round for most gardeners. But if you want to dry larger quantities, cut back the entire plant just before it flowers, leaving 3 to 4 inches of growth at the bottom. The plant will regrow. Hang the sprigs upside down in a dark but ventilated room. Strip the leaves when they are dry and place them in a clean jar for storage.

Common Problem

After a few years, a thyme plant will become woody and the quality of the leaves will decline. Plan to replace your thyme plant every few years for a steady supply of high-quality, fragrant leaves.

Chapter 5: Common Problems and How to Avoid Them

Some people are gifted in gardening. For the rest of us, it takes a little learning and patience to develop intuitive gardening skills. Thankfully, indoor gardening is quite forgiving if you are attentive and notice problems that are beginning with your plants before they have the opportunity to grow into significant issues. We all know that there are problems common in outdoor gardens. Some of the potential problems with indoor gardens are slightly different. While outside growing conditions are certainly never perfect, much of the time, the conditions can correct themselves naturally or with a gentle human nudge. With indoor gardening, we need to recreate what occurs naturally outside of our walls and produce an environment in which plants can thrive. Below is the list of the most usually encountered problems with indoor kitchen gardens and what you can do to solve them and turn a potential gardening disaster into a success.

Abiotic Problems

Abiotic refers to the condition of the environment surrounding the plant, such as the quality and quantity of light, water, and air. Here are common problems that are a result of improper environmental conditions.

Poor Lighting Conditions

Some garden plants require up to eight hours of sunlight a day, while others need only a couple of hours for growth. Providing too much or too little sunlight for plants can result in a list of complications that include:

- Delayed or unproductive flowering and fruit (not enough or the wrong type of light)
- Weak, spindly looking plants (not enough light)
- Slow or weak growth (not enough light)
- Leaves that look dried or scorched (too much direct light)

- Discolored leaves (not enough light)

The solutions to these problems are simple and involve adjusting the amount of direct sunlight that the plant receives. A common misconception is that since most houseplants grow successfully in an indoor environment without much thought that garden plants will as well. While it is true that you can successfully grow many garden plants inside, sometimes you need to make adjustments for their extra need for sunlight. This can be done by changing their location to a southern-facing window with ample sun exposure or purchasing grow lights and using them to supplement natural sunlight.

Hydration Problems

Just like with sunlight, plants can be very particular about how much water they need to thrive. Some plants like moist soil, while others prefer their soil to be more on the dry side. Over or under watering garden plants produces a unique set of symptoms that can include;

- Yellowing leaves (too much water)
- Brown or darkened leaf tips (not enough water)

- Inadequate growth (too much or too little water, sometimes due to root rot)
- General wilted appearance (too much or too little water)

If you find you are having any of these issues with your plants, feel the soil and examine the drainage quality of the container that your plant is in. Each plant should have adequate drainage. This means drainage holes at the bottom of the box and a layer of pebbles or other drainage material in the container's bottom below the soil. If you are having trouble keeping your plants adequately watered, consider purchasing an inexpensive automatic watering system. Also, it is worth taking a look at the air quality and humidity levels in your gardening space. Air that is too humid will contribute to overly wet soil. At the same time, not enough humidity might suck the moisture out of your plants prematurely.

Temperature

For best results, indoor garden plants need to be kept at a temperature that is comparable to the climate that they would be exposed to if they were outside. In most cases, plants will thrive between the range of 75°F to

85°F, with a median temperature of about 80°F being the most favorable. Signs that your plants are suffering from being exposed to improper temperatures include:

- Brown leaf tips
- Yellowing leaves
- Defoliation

You can help regulate the temperature of your plants by placing them on a garden heating mat that can be set to maintain a specific temperature. It is best not to substitute household items such as heating pads and electric blankets because of the potential fire hazard of keeping them on for extended periods.

Too Much Fertilizer

Some fertilizer is a good thing; too much fertilizer is a bad thing. An abundance of nitrogen fertilizer can damage plants, rather than encourage their growth. Signs that you could be using too much fertilizer are:

Browning leaves

Plants that overgrow without producing flowers or fruits

The best way to know how much fertilizer to use for your plants is to ask a professional about each plant species, making sure to mention that you are an indoor gardener. Rather than use chemical fertilizers, try sticking to organic or composted fertilizers, including ones made from ordinary household scraps such as organic vegetable material and coffee grounds.

Indoor Gardening Infections and Bacteria

One of the benefits of indoor gardening over outdoor gardening is that, in general, plants grown indoors are relatively healthy and free from disease and pests. This doesn't mean that they are never encountered, however. Plants that are stressed due to poor growing conditions or lack of attentive care are especially susceptible to infections and bacteria. Following are a few of the most common indoor garden infections that you might encounter.

Root and Stem Rot

When plants are overwatered or are not allowed adequate drainage, the opportunity arises for a disease known as root or stem rot. The symptoms of this disease include;

- Soft stems
- Wilted plants

- Decay
- Soft roots, sometimes foul-smelling
- Dark ring on the stem near the soil

The best treatment for root or stem rot is prevention by not overwatering and providing good drainage for your plants. When you see signs of root or stem rot, remove the infected roots, and transfer the plant to clean fresh soil in a new pot.

Mold and Mildew

Occasionally, you may notice that some of your leaves have powdery appearing mildew substances on them. This is a disease that typically can be caught and remedied before it does too much damage to the plant. Signs of a mold or mildew infection include:

- Powdery white or greenish substance appearing on one or multiple leaves

Drooping leaves

To remedy this condition, it is vital to remove all of the infected parts of the plant and transplant them into fresh soil if the existing ground seems to retain too much moisture. Also, you might want to increase the air circulation around the plant by opening windows or turning on a fan to promote the movement of air. Also, make sure that the soil moisture level remains at a level that is not overly saturated.

Leaf Spots

These tiny spots on leaves caused by different fungus and bacteria can damage the leaves to the point that parts of the plant begin to deteriorate. If your plants are suffering from such a condition, you will notice:

- Brown or yellow spots on leaves
- Spots surrounded by what appears to be a halo
- Spots on the leaves that appear to be saturated with wetness

To solve the issue of spots on your leaves, remove the infected leaves and prevent further infection by avoiding spraying or misting anything on the leaves and improving air circulation in the area around the plants.

Chapter 6: Useful Tips

When it comes to gardening, there are a great many errors that growers are prone to making, when they start out. In fact, truth to tell, many gardeners continue to make mistakes despite having acquired years of experience. The most common reason that mistakes are made is due to ignorance. Some people simply think that if they can raise carrots, then they can raise lettuce; or if they can grow an orange tree, then they understand how to take care of mint. This attitude ignores the subtle (and not so subtle) differences between plants, and simply reduces a vast topic into too-rigid a formula. When this happens, dead plants and poor harvests are prone to follow.

1. Every plant is different, and this means that every plant has different needs, though some elements of those needs may be similar to others. Even within a particular kind of plant, the various subspecies may have vastly different environmental needs compared to each other.

2. Researching should be the first step you take before starting with any new plants. There are a great many questions that you should ask when you are first considering planting a type of plant that you have not worked with before. These can often be answered by researching these questions on Google, or through approaching a knowledgeable employee at your local gardening center.

3. Beginners often aim big and plant all sorts of different plants, with the intention of enjoying them on their dinner plate in the near future. What they overlook is the difficulty associated with maintaining multiple types of plants

simultaneously, and how much time and energy it takes to look after a full garden.

4. It is always smarter to start with 1-3 plants and to bring them from seed to harvest, before branching out and increasing the size of your garden. A modest beginning will give you a sense of how much effort it takes to properly grow your fruits, vegetables, or herbs.

5. When you have your plants too close together, their roots begin to fight each other for nutrients. This wastes energy that would be better employed in growing healthy adult plants. Planting too close together will leave you with small, sickly plants. Planting too close together also makes it easier for pests and diseases to spread from one plant to another. They will not need to travel as far, and there are more parts of the plants that are obscured from the scrutiny of the gardener.

6. Signs like discoloration, bumps, or holes in your leaves are telltale signs of either infestation or infection. Many pests can be tricky to spot if you

are not specifically looking for them and, if left untreated, they can kill your plants.

7. Check the soil and the bottom of your leaves to see if any pests are hiding where you cannot see them. Make it a habit to check daily. Infection can spread quickly through a plant, and any infected leaves or branches should be cut off and disposed of outdoors. Dead plant matter around the growing space can introduce harmful bacteria into the environment. You should always clean up and tidy your growing area every day, washing your hands afterward, before you touch your plants again.

Pest and Disease Management

Pests are not things to joke with, as they are always very harmful to living things of different species, from humans to animals and plants. There are very many types of pests. While we may be very used to a few of them, others are not very common. They come in different shapes and sizes, from termites to rodents, insects, fungus, fleas, to feral dogs. They are simply those living things that threaten humans and their environments, stock, or food.

Luckily, it is not difficult to control pests as there are many ways to go about pest control. If you cannot get rid of them, you can reduce their presence in your farm or living environment. Generally, healthy hygiene is the first step to take when trying to control pests. Having your garden close to a dumpster is the first recipe for pests. Even after the dumpster has been moved, you may want to do critical sanitization before starting your garden. It is no news that refuses sites are quick to accumulate insects, rodents, and other pests. You also do not want to have a pool, stagnant water in your garden. Objects like old tires, abandoned water cans, and so on lying around in your garden are also not a good idea.

There is no doubt that you must control pests in your physical environment, your garden, or your workplace. You don't want your family to contract diseases from pests or from pest-infested foods from your garden, just the same way you may not want your plants to be killed by pests. There is no room for compromise here; the health of humans and their foods is critical, to you have to get your pest control measures right.

Methods of Pest Control

Proper Knowledge: You will get frustrated if you think you will have it comfortable fighting with something you know little or nothing about. This is why you must learn about the pests in your garden, their characteristics, and their effects on your plants. When you grasp the nature of the problems you are dealing with, you can create strategies around defeating them. This is one crucial area where you cannot afford to make mistakes as you don't want to develop wrong strategies that may have ripple effects on your plants' health later. Find those areas in your garden infiltrated by these pests and the damages they can cause or have already caused. The good news is that there are now companies dedicated to helping farmers identify problems, their habitat, and their effects. If you think you cannot easily find pests on your own, you can use such companies' services as they will help you curb the potential damages of such problems and help you avoid their further growth or spread.

Chemical Control: This is the pest control method whereby chemical pesticides are used to get rid of diseases, weeds, or pests. This is simply a way of using toxic or poisonous materials/substances on target pests. When these chemical substances are used, plant protection products are also necessary to shield the plants from their harmful effects. This is very important so that the plants don't end up dying with the pests that you are trying to get rid of.

These days, there are many chemical pesticides used in gardens and even dwelling places to get rid of pests. You must always bear in mind that pesticides are dangerous as they can poison the land, food, water, and air. As a matter of fact, pesticides are as harmful to the persons or people applying them as they are to the pests they are to control. The same goes for every other living thing that is close to the area where the pesticide is applied.

There are five different groups of pesticides. They are grouped according to the work they do. There are fungicides, chemicals used to combat fungi, while herbicides are used to get rid of weeds. This pesticide is either applied to the leaves or the weed roots to kill them. Another category of pesticides is insecticides, which, according to the name, are used to kill dangerous insects. There are acaricides, chemicals that are used to guard plants against mites. The last type of pesticides is known as nematicides, used in controlling nematodes that are harmful to plants. Nematicides are used to combat dangerous animals. They are injected through the mouth, inhaled via breathing, or via what is known as a dermal entry, an entrance through the skin.

Before you use any of these pesticides, make sure you go through the instruction on the pack or container to avoid food poisoning or contact with utensils or other items that may lead to poisoning. It isn't abnormal to find it hard to apply pesticides by yourself. If you find yourself in such a condition, don't hesitate to call pest control experts to help you do the work.

Mechanical Control: There's another pest control method, which involves machines and devices to get rid of pests from the garden. This method is known as automatic control. The most common way of carrying out this method is to create a demarcation between the plant and the insect or pest. This is like the physical method of getting rid of and attacking problems to stop their spread and stop them from causing more damage to the plant. The first step to take in this method is removing all items or factors that may cause the spread of pests. Things like garbage where problems gather to find food or shelter until the coast is clear enough for them to attack the garden should be kept far from the park. You may also want to find solutions to potholes, stagnant water, or other water bodies where pests are likely to gather.

Poisoned Bait: Recall that pests are not just insects. There are rodents and other types of problems, but pest control is used to control insects. This is simply a method where rodents are fed poisoned foods. While this method may be very useful in getting rid of rodents, it may also be hazardous because there's the risk of other more giant animals feeding on the poisoned rodents. When they do, they also get poisoned. There've been cases of people who die because they came in contact with poisoned meat or consumed the meat of poisoned animals. If you must adopt this method, you have to be extremely careful as slight mistakes can turn fatal.

Field Burning: This is one of the oldest forms of pest control. It is usually done after harvest, and it involves the burning of the entire field to destroy all the harmful animals and other species as well as the eggs they may have left behind. This method of pest control sanitizes the area to the core.

Trap Cropping: This is one of the most technical methods there are and involves planting trap crops, plants that attract pests so that they are kept away from other plants. With this method, problems gather around the trap crops, so it is easier to control them in one spot using different methods of pest control like pesticides.

Natural Methods of Pest Control

As years go by, gardeners and farmers become more and more concerned about popular, traditional pest control methods as most of them indicate interest in more natural, eco-friendly methods of pest control. While more people are becoming interested in these pest control methods, the question on most people's minds is whether natural ways of pest control work. The truth remains that when done correctly, natural methods of pest control maybe even more effective than popular pesticides. Most professional pest control organizations realize this fact. They opt for procedures like extremely cold or hot temperatures to get rid of insects like bedbugs. There are many types of natural pest control, as there are many ways of adopting these pest control techniques. Here are a few of them:

Organic Method

If you want healthy pest control methods to combat pests without destroying your plants and animals effectively, choose natural organic forms. This is simply a way of using adequate and sufficient predator baits to eliminate pests. The most organic method of pest control is using sodium fluoroacetate. This biodegradable poison is usually mixed with tricks or traps to eliminate very many types of pests. This is also the cheapest method of pest control for highly infected areas. Other forms of organic pest control are highlighted below:

Floating row covers: Floating row covers are used to control different types of pests like aphids, cabbage worms, tomato hornworms, potato beetles, cabbage moths, squash bugs, and many other moving pests. These covers further protect the plants against predators like squirrels, birds, deer, rabbits, etc. They simply shield the plants without causing any harm to them as they also serve as ways of protecting the plants from strong winds and harsh sun. These floating row covers are the most effective ways of protecting vegetables from many types of pests during those times when problems are most potent and can damage the plants. If you have planted crops that don't undergo insect pollination phases, you may leave the row covers for as long as the plant remains in the garden.

Floating row covers reach very far in protecting your plants. You may choose to spread your material over the plants or support the materials with wires or hoops. They can be wrapped around the cages of plants like the tomato plant to shield them. You only have to remember that you need to keep the sides covered so that the pests cannot reach your plants. Once you have dropped the material over the plants, get rocks or boards to hold the edges tightly. If you want to do this more effectively, use the row covers immediately after planting the crops and leaving them there for as long as you believe necessary.

Insecticidal Soaps: You can use insecticidal soaps to save the lives of your crops when soft-bodied pests suddenly infest your garden. These soaps work best on soft-bodied pests like spider mites, aphids, and whiteflies. The soaps take effect by using fatty acid to destroy the cuticles that serve as a shield to insects. Once these cuticles are broken down, the insect gets dehydrated, and they die. For this process to be effective, the soap has to have physical contact with the insect. As the plant continues to produce new leaves or fruits, you have to repeat this process. This is usually between the space of 5 to 7 days.

Before you apply insecticidal soaps to the leaves, make sure that the plant leaves are all wet on both sides. Note that many harsh soaps may cause the plant's leaves to burn, so you have to carefully test every plant to know the types of insecticidal soaps they can accommodate before pouring the soap on all your crops. The soaps are usually sold in their concentrated forms, so they have to be diluted before they are applied. The diluted form of the insecticidal soaps can only last for a few days, so be careful to mix the quantity that is enough for a single application at a time.

Oil Sprays: Oil sprays are also useful in getting rid of pests. One of the most common types of oil sprays used for this purpose is neem oil, which controls different types of beetles and squash bugs. This oil has many natural steroids, so when they are sprayed on the pests, they become less interested in laying eggs. They lose appetite, so their growth is stunted.

Conclusion

Wow! There aren't many words to say besides congratulations at this point! I am sure that your head is swimming with dozens of little facts concerning plants and when to plant them and how to plant them.

If you already have a plan, I hope this guide gave you some great tips on expansion, and the best vegetables to grow. Granted, you learn a lot through doing, but having adequate information can make it easier for you to avoid simple mistakes from the beginning or be aware of what to look out for.

At this point, you should have a basic understanding of vegetable gardening, what goes into building one, how it works to maintain your plants, and the best type of plants to start off planting in your garden. That's a lot of information! Has anyone told you they're proud of you for getting this far in your vegetable gardening journey? Because I am proud of you!

I encourage you to keep this guide and circle back to it when you need references for some items. For example, if you ever decide to expand you currently have, this guide offers some great things to keep in mind before moving forward with an expansion. You can grow with your plants in knowledge, but there will always be something good about coming back to the basics.

I hope that you can now tell your tomatoes apart from your strawberries and that all the finer parts of the greenhouse make sense to you. It doesn't matter if you're using a greenhouse box or an entire greenhouse that feeds a family or a city, you will continue to learn as you plant every day.

This book focused on imparting the correct vegetable gardening knowledge to you and allowing you to be empowered to construct your own garden. Garden kits can easily be bought from gardening companies or hardware stores and built yourself as well! Practice your building skills and if you run into trouble call the experts for some advice. The best way to know all the ins and outs of your garden is to be present for every decision from what hardware you use to build the vegetable garden, to how exactly it is put together. Remember to leave yourself the option to expand if you need to.

You got an overall sense of what you could begin to plant in your garden. Ultimately, this is a personal decision, fueled by how much time you have to dedicate to your garden, the climate you keep in your greenhouse, and the types of fruits and vegetables that your family likes to eat.

Hopefully, this guide carries you into some productive planting and growing! There's a lot to learn when it comes to gardening. Good luck and happy growing!